Every rock tells a story from the earth's past. This book will show you how to read rocks and unlock their secrets.

Shown here are magnetite and sandstone from Wyoming, rose quartz from South Dakota, pumice from New Mexico, and slate from Colorado.

ROCKS AND MINERALS

LeeAnn Srogi

Running Press • Philadelphia, Pennsylvania

Canadian representatives: General Publishing Co., Ltd., 30 Lesmill Road, Don Mills, Ontario M3B 2T6.

International representatives: Worldwide Media Services, Inc., 115 East Twenty-third Street, New York, NY 10010.

9 8 7 6 5 4 3 2 1
Digit on the right indicates the number of this printing.

Library of Congress Cataloging-in-Publication Number
88–42746   ISBN 0–89471–675–1

Cover design by Toby Schmidt
Interior illustration by Helen I. Driggs

Introduction to Chapter 3, page 26, adapted from *The Letters of the Younger Pliny* (pp. 171–72), translated by Betty Radice (Penguin Classics, 1963, 1969), copyright © 1963, 1969 by Betty Radice. Reproduced by permission of Penguin Books Ltd.

Photograph on page 74 courtesy of the National Gallery of Art: *Rock Settees,* 1988, by Scott Burton, born 1939; National Gallery of Art, Gift of the Collectors Committee.

Photographs courtesy of the Smithsonian Institution:
    Department of Anthropology, p. 79, cat. no. 204154, neg. no. 84-14501; p. 83, cat. no. 148149, neg. no. 75-6648 (top), neg. no. 76-3319 (bottom); p. 85, cat. nos. 207909, 207910, 207911, 207938, neg. no. 78-8220 (bottom); p. 94, cat. no. 274032, neg. no. 85-16233.
    Museum of Natural History: p. 11 (bottom), p. 12, neg. no. 12047 (top); p. 13, neg. no. 32479-C; p. 16, neg. nos. 148268, 145166; p. 29, neg. no. 2923B; p. 30, neg. no. 76-4018 (bottom); p. 31, neg. no. R-132-5; p. 56, neg. no. MNH 354; p. 57; p. 58, neg. no. 32478-0; p. 59, neg. no. 38181-A; p. 60, neg. no. MNH 384; p. 61, neg. nos. 38182 (top), MNH 939A (bottom); p. 78, neg. nos. 36474-C (left), 32478-H (right); p. 81, neg. no. 79-9881; p. 82, neg. no. 32814-A; p. 84, neg. no. 77-12984; p. 85, neg. no. 42883 (top); p. 86; p. 90, neg. no. 81-2088 14A.
    National Museum of American History: p. 12, neg. no. 801697 (bottom); p. 34, neg. no. 75-798; p. 53, neg. no. 74-2657; p. 77, neg. no. 72-4510.

Photographs courtesy of the U.S. Geological Survey: p. 20, neg. no. 1 by E.A. Cernan; p. 27, neg. no. 16 by R.G. Luedke; p. 30, neg. no. 1413 by N.H. Darton (top); p. 32 by Ross Hamilton; p. 33, neg. no. 551 by K. Segerstrom (top); p. 38, neg. no. PIO-88-49A by R.E. Wallace; p. 48, neg. no. 413, Earthquake Information Bulletin; p. 50, neg. no. 67 by G.H. Goudarzi; p. 54, neg. no. 280 by W.T. Schaller; p. 55, neg. no. 174 by W.T. Schaller; p. 57, neg. no. 92 by C.E. Dobbin; p. 58, neg. no. 680 by D.B. Sterrett; p. 63, neg. no. 91 by J.B. Eby; p. 64, neg. no. 50 by P.T. Hayes (top), neg no. 126 by E.S. Bastin; p. 65, neg. no. 3 by D.A. Swanson; p. 66, neg. no. 2 by C. Milton; p. 67, neg. no. 53 by P.T. Hayes; p. 68, neg. no. 12 by R.L. Parker; p. 70, neg. no. 115 by T.N. Dale; p. 100, neg. no. 144 by W.R. Hanson; p. 101, neg. no. 321 (bottom); p. 103, neg. no. 352; p. 104, neg. no. 425; p. 105, neg. no. 1133 by H.E. Malde.

Photographs courtesy of the American Museum of Natural History, Department of Library Services: p. 11, neg. no. K5302 (top and center) ; p. 33, neg. no. 3133 (Photo by R. Weber); p. 66, neg. no. 120045 (left) (Photo by Thane Bierwert); p. 88, neg. no. 117704 (top) (Photo by J. Kirschner); neg. no. K11200 (bottom).

Photographs courtesy of AP/Wide World Photos, p. 35; AT&T Archives, p. 93; The Bettmann Archive, pp. 26, 37, 62 (Photo by H.H. Turner, USGS 111), 76, 87, 95-97, 106; GE Research and Development Center, pp. 15, 99; NASA, p. 19; New York State Department of Economic Development, pp. 69, 89; Texas Instruments Incorporated, p. 98; Western Pennsylvania Conservancy, p. 14 (Photo by Harold Corsini) ; Woods Hole Oceanographic Institution, p. 101 (top) by Rod Catanach, p. 102 by Kathleen Crane.

Printed in the United States of America by Port City Press, Baltimore, MD
Typography by COMMCOR Communications Corporation, Philadelphia, PA

This book may be ordered by mail from the publisher. Please add $2.50 for postage and handling. *But try your bookstore first!*

Running Press Book Publishers
125 South Twenty-second Street
Philadelphia, Pennsylvania 19103

For Frankie and Gee Srogi

Acknowledgments
I would like to thank Tim Lutz, Ian
Harker, Bob Giegengack, and Charlie
Thayer for their help, advice, and
references; and Steve Zorn for his
splendid editing and cheerful
patience.

Contents

Introduction

Did you know that . . .

. . . the highest mountain on earth is mostly underwater.
The highest mountain is the Island of Hawaii, which is the largest of the Hawaiian Islands. Hawaii is a cluster of five volcanos, two of which are still active. When the volcanos erupted, molten rock was spewed from inside the earth. This liquid rock hardened as it cooled, forming the island.

. . . thin slices of quartz crystal tell time in digital watches.
In a digital watch, an electric current produced by a small battery causes a very thin slice of quartz to vibrate rapidly at a precise rate. An electronic circuit counts how many times the quartz vibrates, and sends a signal to the watch display.

. . . stones from space tell us what's inside the earth.
The shooting stars you sometimes see in the night sky are pieces of early planets in our solar system. Those that survive their fall to earth are meteorites. By studying meteorites, geologists are learning more about the history of the rocks and minerals near the center of the earth.

. . .diamonds form about 150 miles within the earth and come to the surface as fast as a jet plane.

Deep inside the earth, heat and pressure are so intense that carbon is transformed into diamonds. The rocks carrying the diamonds are forced upward by escaping gas and molten rock, reaching speeds up to 700 miles an hour.

Our planet earth is full of marvels like these. With this book, you'll explore the earth as you start collecting a vast assortment of rocks and minerals. You'll learn what minerals, crystals, and rocks are, where to find them, and how to identify them.

But there's more. A glimpse into human history will show you how people have depended upon metals, minerals, and rocks for thousands of years, from stone-age tools to spaceships.

Here's a guided tour of our planet, with some of the latest ideas about what it's made of and how it works.

CHAPTER 1

Animal, Vegetable, or Mineral?

One of the most familiar minerals is ice – and its crystals are some of the most beautiful of all, as the two snowflakes above show. The crystal below may look like a snowflake, but it's the metal zinc, enlarged thousands of times by an electron microscope.

Before you head off on a rock-and-mineral hunt, look around your home. You can find rocks and minerals in some unexpected places.

If you open the freezer you'll find a mineral there: it's found in nature and it has a crystal form, so scientists call ice a mineral. Snowflakes are six-sided crystals of ice. If you could take an X ray of an ice cube, you would see that it has the same crystal structure as a snowflake. Is water also a mineral? A geologist would say it's not, because it's liquid, and minerals are solid.

You'll find minerals in all shapes and sizes – from fibers and needles to chunks. They can be almost any color.

Some are hard; others are very soft. Still, all minerals have a few things in common. Minerals are always solid and are found in nature, but they aren't made by living things.

Table salt (or halite) is an important mineral whose crystals form little cubes. Salt is mined from deposits that formed as the water of ancient seas evaporated. More than 1,000 feet below the city of Detroit are abandoned salt mines that formed when an inland sea dried up about 400 million years ago.

If salt is a mineral, what about sugar? Salt and sugar look the same, but sugar is not a mineral because it is extracted from living things – plants.

When it's found in rocks, apatite is called a mineral. But when it forms in teeth and bones, it's considered a mineraloid. This mineral sample was found in Maine.

Some substances are identical to minerals in every way except that they are not formed in the earth. These substances are called *mineraloids*. For example, you can find a mineral called apatite in many rocks. Its crystals are shiny with a blue, green, or golden color. Your bones and teeth contain a substance which is identical to apatite, except that it forms inside your body instead of inside a rock. Some geologists study mineraloids in bones and teeth and kidney stones just as they would study the minerals in a rock.

Magnets like the ones you may have on your refrigerator can be called mineraloids. These are synthetic minerals made in laboratories, and are very similar to a natural magnetic mineral called magnetite. Both are made of iron and oxygen. Many centuries ago, small pieces of magnetic magnetite, called lodestone, were used in compasses. Now, magnetized metal is used.

The needle on this antique surveyor's compass is a sliver of steel that was magnetized by rubbing it against a lodestone, a natural magnet made of the mineral magnetite.

A group of minerals once common in homes and other buildings is known as asbestos. Asbestos forms thin, flexible fibers. Because it is fireproof, it was used as insulation and fabric until it was discovered that the tiny fibers could drift into the air and harm the lungs of people who breathed them. Today, synthetic materials are substituted for asbestos.

The softest mineral known is one you may find around your home: talc. When talc is ground and mixed with perfume and other substances it becomes talcum powder.

Other minerals are prized for their hardness. Tiny grains of garnet or corundum, two of the hardest minerals known, are used to make the rough surface of sandpaper.

Its downy fibers once made asbestos a popular material for insulation, but some forms of this mineral are harmful to breathe.

Rocks Around the Block

Rocks and stones are made of one or more minerals. In fact, rocks are a little like a salad: just as a salad is a mix of several vegetables, a rock is a mix of minerals. The rock called granite, for example, is made of the minerals quartz, feldspar, amphibole, and mica.

The minerals in a rock are held together in many ways. Sometimes they fit together like the pieces of a jigsaw puzzle. Sometimes one mineral acts like glue, filling the spaces and cementing the rock together.

You can find rocks and minerals all around your neighborhood. The rocks you see in nearby buildings may tell

Named Fallingwater by its architect, Frank Lloyd Wright, this house is made of sandstone quarried at the construction site in Western Pennsylvania. The white balcony and roof are concrete. Now a museum, this is an interesting example of a fieldstone house built in harmony with its surroundings.

you something about the area where you live. Anywhere you see houses made of stone, you can guess that the stones probably came from within a few miles of the house. Early in this country's history, farmers pried stones out of their fields to clear the land for farming and used the stones to build their homes and the fireplaces that warmed them. That's where the name fieldstone comes from.

Concrete sidewalks and driveways are also made of rocks. Look for small pebbles in the concrete, each of which is a little piece of rock. The concrete mixture is held together by a gray or whitish cement, made from a rock called limestone. To make cement, limestone is mixed with clay and heated. After being mixed with sand, gravel, and water, it hardens to form concrete.

Some rocks occur naturally in rich deposits, but only in certain places. The most famous marble comes from Carrara, in central Italy, but Vermont also produces excellent varieties. Most marble used in floors is polished to reveal its beautiful colors and patterns, but unpolished marble is often used to make outdoor stairs and doorsteps.

It's Elementary!

What do the dull gray lead in a pencil and a sparkling diamond have in common? You may have guessed that they're both minerals, but what's surprising is that they're both made of the element called carbon.

Elements are the purest forms of matter. Every atom is an element, and everything in the universe is made up of just 103 elements, which can combine with each other or exist by themselves. Carbon is one of these elements.

How can a diamond, which is crystal clear and the hardest substance

This pile of black powder is a diamond in the rough. It's graphite, a mineral of carbon that's used to make pencil leads and synthetic diamonds, like the ones shown here.

on earth, and graphite, the soft, slippery material used to make pencil leads, both be made of pure carbon? The reason they're so different is that they form in different parts of the earth. Diamonds can only form deeper than 100 miles below the earth's surface, where heat and tremendous pressure shape carbon into diamond.

Graphite forms in rocks that are not buried so deeply, where the heat and pressure aren't so great.

Although diamond and graphite are both made of carbon, they are different minerals, with different colors, different properties, and different crystal structures.

When Is a Crystal a Mineral?

All minerals can develop a crystal form if conditions are right, but not every crystal can be considered a mineral.

A crystal is solid and has an orderly arrangement of atoms forming smooth, flat faces. Crystals can be transparent or opaque, and they can be any color or size.

A crystal can be formed naturally in the earth (such as a diamond), manufactured (such as cubic zirconia), or produced by a plant or animal (such as sugar).

A mineral is found only in nature, and is produced only by non-living things; a mineral made in a laboratory is called a *synthetic mineral*.

Crystals are not living things; they "grow" as more and more atoms are attached to their surfaces. The crystal faces develop only if there is enough space for the atoms to arrange themselves properly. Some substances, like the mineral quartz, form crystals that always look about the same. Other solids form a variety of crystal shapes. Crystals of the mineral calcite can be found in more than 300 different shapes.

Crystals can form in many beautiful shapes – from pompons of needle-like mesolite (top) to flaky wedges of barite (left).

Growing Crystals

You can grow small crystals at home, using salt, sugar, or powdered alum, available in most drugstores.

You'll need:
- a large drinking glass or wide-mouthed glass jar, taller than it is wide
- boiling water
- 1 to 3 cups of salt, sugar, or powdered alum (choose one)
- string
- a pencil or stick, longer than the glass is wide
- a paper clip
- a paper towel

Fill the container about three-quarters full of boiling water. Add the salt, or sugar, or alum, a spoonful at a time, and stir until it dissolves. Keep adding more, and keep stirring, until there's just a little at the bottom that won't dissolve. You may need to add a lot of material and stir for a while.

Tie the end of the string to the middle of the pencil. The string should just touch the bottom of the container when you balance the pencil across the opening. If the string floats, attach a paper clip to the end of it.

Put the container in a dry, draft-free place where it won't be disturbed. Drape a paper towel loosely over it to keep out dust, and wait for the water to evaporate.

In a few days, you'll see a cluster of crystals along the string, at the bottom, and on the walls of the container. The crystals interfere with each other as they grow, but notice how all the crystals have the same basic shape, regardless of their different sizes.

The longer you let the crystals stay in the liquid, the larger they'll "grow." Once the crystals stop growing, you can remove the crystal-covered string from the liquid and let it dry on a paper towel.

Try growing crystals of different substances to see how their shapes vary.

CHAPTER 2

The Birth of the Earth

What does the earth look like?

The ancient Greeks thought that the world rested on the shoulders of a giant named Atlas. The Huron Indians of North America believed the world sat on a tortoise's back. In medieval Europe, many believed that the earth was flat, like a tabletop.

The voyages of Magellan and other explorers who sailed around the world finally persuaded them that the world is round. Today, satellite pictures taken from space show us that our planet looks like a ball covered with blue oceans and swirling clouds.

The earth and eight other planets formed around the star we call the sun between 4½ and 5 billion years ago. The most recent scientific theory suggests that a rotating cloud of gas and dust collapsed to form the sun and planets. No one knows why the gaseous cloud collapsed, but one possibility is that a nearby supernova—a violently exploding star—triggered the process. As the gaseous cloud collapsed, the center reached a temperature of more than one million degrees Fahrenheit, forming our sun. As the cloud of gas and dust cooled, the first minerals were formed. They came together to make up earth and the other eight planets of our solar system.

Beneath the serene face of the earth, rocks are being created and folded together, continents are shifting, and molten rock is rising to the surface.

By studying rocks brought back from the moon, scientists are learning about the earth and our solar system.

The earth's early atmosphere was poor in oxygen and rich in carbon dioxide compared with today's atmosphere; we owe the life-sustaining air we breathe to the blue-green bacteria which evolved on the young earth. These bacteria, like the green plants we see today, take carbon dioxide from the air and give off oxygen as waste. Over hundreds of millions of years, our atmosphere became oxygen-rich, and it is now sustained by the green plants that live on land and in the oceans.

What's on the Surface?

The earth is almost (but not quite) a perfect sphere just about 25,000 miles (about 40,000 kilometers) around at the equator. The distance from its surface to the center is about 3,950 miles (about 6,370 kilometers).

The interior of the earth has three parts, one inside the other. The central part is the core; the next part, which is the largest section, is the mantle; and the outer portion is the crust.

The rocks you find around you were formed in the crust or the top portion of the earth's mantle. The earth's crust is less than 60 miles thick at its deepest point and it accounts for less than 1 percent of the earth's weight. The crusts of the moon and Mars are much thicker, and make up 10 percent of the weight of those heavenly bodies.

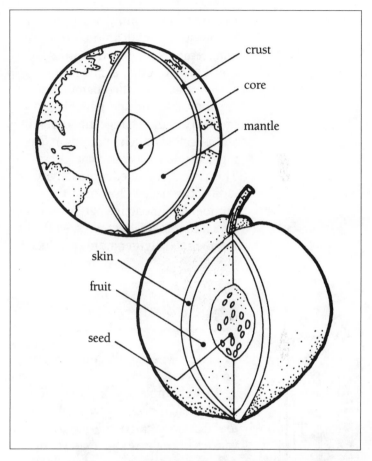

The earth's crust is less than 60 miles thick in most places – not very thick at all, considering the earth's size. For example, if a plum were as large as the earth, its skin would be close to 200 miles thick.

Clocks in Rocks

Geologists determine the age of rocks by measuring small amounts of certain elements produced by the breakdown of other elements.

Some atoms, called parent atoms, are not stable and spontaneously break apart and change into different atoms, called daughter atoms, releasing heat and energy in the process. This process is called radioactivity or radioactive decay. Over time, the number of radioactive parent atoms in a rock or mineral decreases, while the number of daughter atoms produced by decay increases. Uranium is probably the most familiar radioactive element. It takes billions of years for uranium to produce daughter atoms of lead.

Each kind of radioactive element decays at its own rate. So, by knowing how fast the parent atoms decay, and by measuring the relative amounts of parent and daughter atoms in a rock, geologists can measure its age. It's a little like having a clock built into a rock, recording the time since the rock formed.

Telling Time

Radioactive decay tells time like an hourglass.

In an hourglass, grains of sand in the top half of the glass gradually fall to the bottom half of the glass. Just as various hourglasses are made with openings of different sizes so that the sand grains pass from the top to the bottom at different rates of speed, each radioactive element has its own unique rate of decay.

Think of it this way: how long will it take for half of the parent atoms to decay into daughter atoms? For the radioactive element carbon 14, it will take 5,570 years. For the element rubidium 87, it will take about 47 billion years. Carbon 14 is used to date more recent materials, and rubidium 87 is used to date rocks more than a few million years old.

How Old Is the Earth?

Clues to the age of the earth come from meteorites – rocks that fall to earth from outer space. Most meteorites are pieces of planets similar to ours, which formed and then broke apart early in the history of the solar system. The oldest meteorites are about 4½ billion years old, and our solar system is even older.

It's hard to imagine a number as big as 4,500,000,000. How many one-gallon buckets would you need to hold 4½ billion grains of sand? You might think that a few dozen bucketfuls would do the job. Actually, more than 1,000 buckets would be needed; 4½ billion is an enormous number.

Geologists have divided the earth's 4½-billion-year history into shorter periods, called eras. This is known as geologic time. Each era in geologic time marks a major change in plants and animals.

Life existed on earth more than three billion years ago, but familiar forms of life did not develop until much more recently. The most important boundary in earth history is the appearance of the first life similar to the plants and animals alive today. These were shellfish, now preserved in rock as fossils, and they appeared about 570 million years ago, at the beginning of the Paleozoic Era. Dinosaurs and early mammals appeared at the beginning of the Mesozoic Era, 245 million years ago. We live in the Cenozoic Era, which began 66 million years ago, when the last of the dinosaurs became extinct.

Plants and animals have changed a great deal over 570 million years, but when you consider the entire lifetime of the earth, 570 million years is not that long ago. If the history of the earth were a book 90 pages long, each page would represent 50 million years. Dinosaurs would appear on page 86 and would still be roaming around at the bottom of the next-to-last page. Humans would not appear until the very bottom of the last page. If you cut one inch from the bottom of the last page of the book, you would remove all humans and their immediate ancestors from earth history.

Make a Geologic Time Line

You can make a geologic time line to illustrate the history of life of the earth. You will need:

- masking tape
- 90″ length of string
- a ruler
- scissors

Colored tape or colored markers will make the time line more attractive.

Wrap a piece of tape around each end of the string, leaving an overlap as a label on which to write. Mark one end of the tape "Birth of the Earth." This is the beginning of the string, indicating the beginning of geologic time. Mark the tape on the other end of the string "Today" or "The Present." Now you can wrap and label tape all along the string to mark important events in earth history. This chart should help get you started.

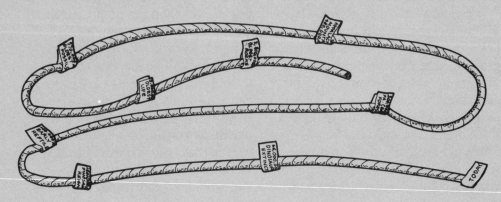

Major feature	When (years ago)	Inches from beginning of string
PRECAMBRIAN ERA		
Oldest known rocks	3,800,000,000	14″
Oldest known life (bacteria)	3,500,000,000	20″
PALEOZOIC ERA		
Oldest fossils like modern plants and animals	570,000,000	78½″
Appalachian Mountains begin to form	480,000,000	80½″
Huge swamps in North America and Europe (now coal)	300,000,000	84″
MESOZOIC ERA		
Dinosaurs reign	150,000,000	87″
Canadian Rocky Mountains form	100,000,000	88″
Dinosaurs extinct	66,000,000	88¾″
CENOZOIC ERA		
Rocky Mountains form in the U.S.	50,000,000	89″
Earliest human ancestors	15,000,000	89¾″
First appearance of modern humans (*Homo sapiens*)	500,000	89⁶³/₆₄″ (too close to the end to measure!)

CHAPTER 3

Reading Rocks

When Vesuvius erupted in 79 A.D., it destroyed the city of Pompeii, burying many of the townspeople and preserving their bodies in rock.

"By dawn the light was still dim and faint. The buildings around us were tottering. . . . That finally decided us to leave the town. We were followed by a panic-stricken mob of people who hurried us on our way by pressing hard behind. . . . The carriages we had ordered brought out began to run in different directions though the ground was quite level, and would not remain stationary even when wedged with stones. We also saw the sea sucked away and apparently forced back by the earthquake; at any rate it receded from the shore so that many sea creatures were left stranded on dry sand. On the landward side a fearsome black cloud was rent by forked and quivering bursts of flame, and parted to reveal great tongues of fire, like flashes of lightning magnified in size.

"Soon afterward the cloud sank down to earth and covered the sea. . . . Then darkness came once more and ashes began to fall again, this time heavily. We rose and shook them off, otherwise we would have been buried and crushed beneath their weight."

— Pliny the Younger, age 18, describing the eruption of Vesuvius, Italy, 79 A.D.

The earth is a restless planet, never still. Water, wind, and ice continually change the surface, while inside the earth, other processes are occurring. Rocks are formed both inside the earth and at its surface.

To classify rocks, geologists arrange them into three categories according to how they were formed.

Wind and water can wear away mountains, turning stone to sand, as you can see in this photograph of Bryce Canyon National Park, Utah.

Sedimentary Rocks

Weather and water can wear away rocks and sculpt mountain valleys, river channels, and sand dunes. This process of erosion breaks down the rocks into little pieces of sediment – sand, mud, dirt, and gravel. Together with the tiny remains of dead plants and animals, these are picked up, carried away, and eventually left behind by rivers and streams, wind, and ice. The sediments that are left behind become sedimentary rocks, the most common kind of rocks. Sedimentary rocks form near the surface of the crust by processes you see happening around you. Watch as a rainstorm sweeps dust and dirt in little streams down the street; look at the ripples in sand left by waves at the beach. Some sediments, like the salt and mineral layers at the bottom of lakes and seas, are left high and dry when the water evaporates. Particles of sediment pile up, and as the ones at the bottom of the pile are weighed down and slowly cemented together by minerals, they gradually turn to stone.

It's easy to recognize sedimentary rocks. Most have horizontal layers of various shades, the result of sediments accumulating over time. Look for fossils, too; these are found almost exclusively in sedimentary rocks.

A Sedimentation Demonstration

In a simple experiment, you can create layered sediments that look like layers of rock.

You'll need:
- a large glass jar with a tight-fitting lid
- a mixture of sand, gravel, and mud
- water

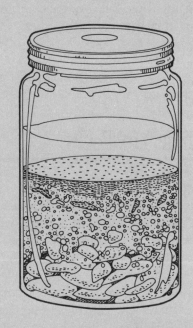

Fill the jar no more than halfway with the sand, gravel, and mud mixture. Add water until the jar is almost full. Cover it and shake hard – but carefully! – to mix the sediments. Then let the jar sit undisturbed for a while. The large, heavy pieces of gravel will settle quickly to the bottom of the jar. The sand will settle more slowly, forming a layer on top of the gravel and filling in between the pebbles. The mud will remain suspended in the water for quite a while, but eventually it will form a very fine layer on top.

The same thing happens when sediments pass from a river into a lake or sea. The sediment carried by the moving water settles out into the more quiet water: first the gravel, then the sand, and finally the mud. Over a long time, sediments build up to form deltas at the mouths of rivers. New Orleans, Louisiana, is built on a huge delta where the Mississippi River empties into the Gulf of Mexico.

What Grows Inside a Rock?

Strange and wondrous rock forms are sometimes found within sedimentary rocks. Lumps of black, gray, or red minerals, called *concretions*, "grow" inside sediments. A grain of sand or a piece of shell acts as a seed for the concretion. As seawater percolates through sediments, like water percolating through coffee grounds, minerals settle out of the seawater and grow in layers around the seed. Concretions are usually made of chert (a form of quartz), but may be made of other minerals as well. Most concretions are round, but some look like turtles or even hands. People once believed that concretions were evil charms.

Another fascinating find is a *geode*, a rounded mass of quartz that is lumpy on the outside and contains agate or quartz crystals in its center. As with the process that forms concretions, a mineral—in this case, crystals of quartz—settles out of water percolating through sediments. Unlike concretions, however, geodes form inside cavities in the sediments (good crystals need plenty of free space in which to grow). Sometimes these cavities appear as a dead plant or animal decays. In this way, a living thing dies and is replaced by a cluster of beautiful crystals.

Sedimentary processes are responsible for forming fossils. When a plant or animal dies and is quickly buried by sediments, the minerals in the sediments replace the cells of the plant or animal as it decomposes. The result is a perfect, stone replica of a once-living thing. When the wood fibers in the trunk of a fallen tree are gradually replaced by quartz, the tree becomes petrified wood.

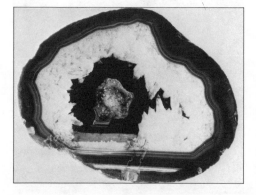

You never know what you'll find inside a geode. This geode is filled with beautiful crystals of quartz.

Sedimentary Specialties

Some of the world's most important ore minerals and gem crystals have been formed in hot water. They form by a hydrothermal (hot water) process. Molten rock underneath a volcano can heat water trapped in rocks close to the surface of the earth. Certain elements, (including silicon, which is found in quartz and thousands of other minerals) and certain compounds containing metals (such as copper and lead), dissolve in the hot water. As the water flows through cracks in the rocks, minerals settle out of the water and form crystals on the sides of the rocks. The same process causes the hard, white mineral deposits that form inside a teakettle.

One of the largest ore deposits formed by the hydrothermal process is a deposit of minerals containing lead and zinc that stretches from Oklahoma to southern Wisconsin. Sedimentary rocks (limestone and dolomite) are encrusted with lead ore (the mineral galena) and zinc ore (the mineral sphalerite). Other metal-bearing minerals also occur along the belt, and in some places beautiful crystals of calcite and fluorite can be found.

They look ordinary enough, but the logs above and the bird's nest at right are made of stone. Minerals slowly replaced the decaying cells of the trees and the eggs, preserving their original shapes in solid rock.

Some types of the mineral fluorite glow in ultraviolet light. Fluorite is often used in manufacturing steel, to lower the melting point of the metal, making it easier to work with.

Inside the Earth

The interior of the earth is made entirely of rocks, and they are *hot*. Mines drilled more than 1,000 feet below the surface are uncomfortably warm, and it gets hotter as you get closer to the center of the earth. The earth is so hot inside that some of it is molten rock, or magma. Just as hot air is lighter than cool air, magma is lighter than the cooler rock around it, and so it tends to rise. Part of the earth's core is entirely molten, but this melted rock is so deep within the earth that it never reaches the surface. However, magma is also produced in small amounts in the upper part of the earth's mantle, less than 150 miles below the surface. Very gradually, some of this magma rises toward the surface.

About 1,300 feet of mountaintop blew off Mount Saint Helens when it erupted in 1980. This volcano, located in southwest Washington, erupts every 150 years or so.

Igneous Rocks

As the magma rises, it cools and the minerals inside it form solid crystals. Eventually, all the melted rock solidifies or crystallizes within the crust of the earth and becomes igneous rock.

After millions of years, these rocks are revealed as the layers of rocks above them (which are usually softer, sedimentary rocks) are worn away. Many of the mountains in New England and eastern California are made of igneous rocks that formed in this way.

When magma reaches the surface of the earth before it cools and becomes solid, it creates a volcano. Magma that flows over the surface of the earth is called lava, and when magma explodes into the air, it forms volcanic ash. As the ash falls to earth it often forms the rock called pumice, which looks a little like a sponge. Pumice is full of tiny air bubbles and is so light that it floats in water. Pumice stones are sold as beauty aids, to rub dry skin from feet and elbows.

Metamorphic Rocks

Inside the earth, rocks are under great pressure from the rocks above them. At 100 miles below the surface of the earth, the pressure is about 600,000 pounds per square inch (psi)—enough to form carbon into diamonds. At the earth's core, the pressure reaches about 29 million psi.

The action of heat, pressure, and massive shifting inside the crust and mantle of the earth often changes igneous and sedimentary rocks into other kinds of rocks, which we call metamorphic rocks. Soft limestone, a sedimentary rock, can be changed into the durable marble used for buildings; particles of clay that make up the sedimentary rock shale, can be metamorphosed into slate.

The record of metamorphic forces can be seen in the folding observed in many metamorphic rocks. These folds look like wrinkles in a rug that has been pushed up along one edge. Imagine how hard you would have to squeeze sedimentary rocks in order to push the straight, flat layers into folds. Does it seem impossible? Incredibly, the forces in the earth, acting over long periods of time, can bend and break rocks as though they were putty.

These limestone rocks have been squeezed and folded by forces below the earth's surface. At lower right, two rockhounds examine the evidence.

This metamorphic rock, called gneiss, is a record of the powerful forces that can bend rock.

How Can We Tell?

Since we can't explore the earth's interior directly, how do we know so much about it?

Most of our information about the earth's interior comes from earthquakes. The earth's crust is cut by numerous faults, large cracks along which the rocks on either side move in opposite directions. These rocks shift very suddenly, producing the ground-shaking motions we feel as earthquakes. Earthquake vibrations travel all the way through the earth and can be detected by machines called seismographs. The vibrations slow down, speed up, or change direction depending on what kind of rock they encounter inside the earth. The behavior of earthquake vibrations, as measured by seismographs all over the world, gives us a picture of what the earth is like inside.

Ancient Chinese seismoscopes, like the model shown here, were used to track earthquakes. Vibrations from a quake would cause the dragon facing in the direction of the quake to drop its marble into the frog's mouth.

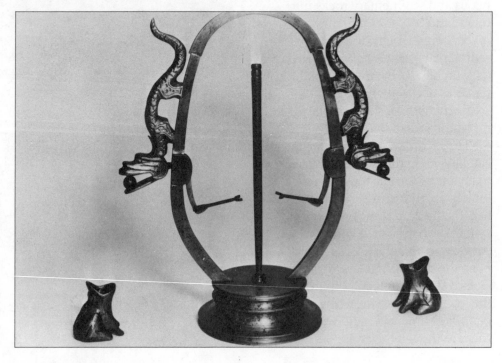

A 1988 earthquake in Armenia, in the U.S.S.R, was one of the worst natural disasters of this century.

The continents and oceans make up enormous plates that float upon semi-rolid rock. When the plates shift, earth-quakes and volcanos result.

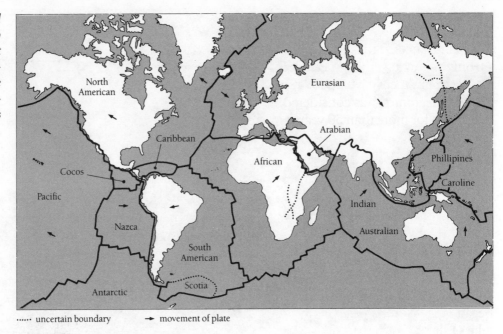

North American

Eurasian

Caribbean

Arabian

Cocos

African

Phillipines

Pacific

Caroline

Nazca

Indian

South American

Australian

Antarctic

Scotia

······ uncertain boundary   → movement of plate

Our Restless Planet

If you look at a map of South America and Africa, doesn't it seem as though the two continents would fit together if the Atlantic Ocean weren't in the way? Many people have noticed this "co-incidence," and in 1915 a German

meteorologist named Alfred Wegener published a book pointing out that the rocks and fossils of eastern South America and western Africa are very similar—so similar, he said, that the two continents must have once been next to each other. Wegener suggested that all the continents had once been joined in a "supercontinent," which broke up only about 200 million years ago.

Wegener's theory, which today we call *plate tectonics,* was considered ridiculous for more than 50 years; even Wegener could not explain how the solid rocks of the continents could move across the surface of the earth. But in the 1950s, startling discoveries seemed to confirm Wegener's theory.

For years, geologists had thought that the ocean floor was made of the oldest rocks on earth, and that the oceans had remained unchanged since early in earth history. But as they began to make measurements and take samples, geologists found that the ocean floors were made of relatively young rocks, no more than about 200 million years old. In fact, the crust that makes up the ocean floor is changing constantly, as magma oozes out of the mantle below. It was discovered that the continents and the ocean floor "float" on a hot, almost liquid layer of rock within the mantle that continually rises, sinks, and moves. In the Atlantic Ocean, as the new ocean floor forms, it actually pushes the continents apart a few inches every year.

Inch by inch, the Atlantic Ocean is growing larger and the Pacific Ocean is

The sensitive needle of a seismograph can record tremors in the earth many miles away. This photo shows a seismograph at the Oregon Museum of Science and Industry reacting to an underground nuclear test in Alaska in 1971.

The Pacific plate and the North American plates grind past each other at the San Andreas fault in the central coastal ranges of California. San Francisco, on the North American plate, and Los Angeles, on the Pacific plate, are slowly sliding toward one another, and could become sister cities several million years from now.

shrinking. The Pacific Ocean is rimmed by deep valleys, or trenches. The deepest part of the ocean is almost seven miles (11 kilometers) deep, in a trench near the Marianas Islands in the southwest Pacific. At the trenches, one piece of ocean crust is dropped down into the mantle beneath another piece of crust.

Sometimes, as the ocean floor shifts, entire oceans disappear. India was once part of Antarctica, far south of its present position. The ocean between India and Asia gradually disappeared as the ocean crust sank into the mantle between the continents. As the water drained into other parts of the ocean, India gradually drifted closer to Asia. When the Indian continent collided with the Asian continent, it formed the high Himalaya Mountains.

Ring of Fire

Something else is happening near the trenches. Along the mountains of the western coast of Central and South America, there are many active volcanos. When the ocean crust sinks back into the mantle, some of the rocks melt to form magma, which rises into the continents to erupt as volcanos. In addition, land masses grinding against one another in trenches produces earthquakes. Some of the world's most violent earthquakes and volcanic eruptions occur near the trenches that encircle the Pacific Ocean, earning this area its nickname, "The Ring of Fire."

In ancient times, sudden eruptions destroyed towns and villages without warning. For many people, the dangers of volcanos are a fact of life. The islands of Hawaii, for example, are made of igneous rocks formed by active volcanos. When Hawaii's most famous volcano, Kilauea, erupted in 1987, many houses were crushed and burned as the hot lava poured over them.

Other volcanos are much more dangerous because they are unpredictable. In 1980, geologists were expecting Mount Saint Helens in Washington State to erupt, but no one foresaw the violent explosion that blew off the whole side of the mountain. Clearly, geologists need to learn more about igneous processes so that they can protect people from volcanic "surprises" as much as possible.

The Rock Cycle

Many rocks you can find contain minerals that were created millions of years ago and that may have traveled miles below the surface of the earth and back again.

The rocks that cover the surface of the earth are gradually shifting in a repeating cycle that carves our continents and shapes our oceans.

The heat inside the earth moves the weak layer of almost-liquid rock within the mantle. The rock in the crust above this layer is broken into segments, called plates, bounded by ridges, trenches, and gigantic faults such as the San Andreas Fault in California, where huge plates grind slowly past one another.

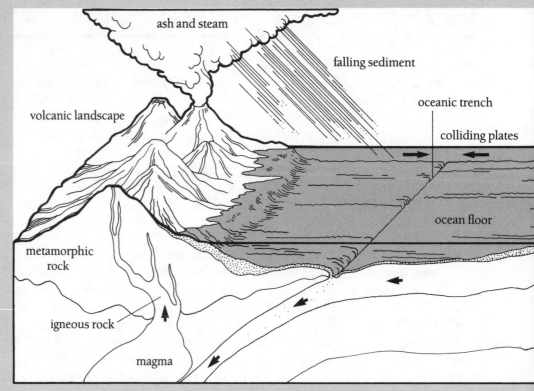

ash and steam

falling sediment

oceanic trench

colliding plates

volcanic landscape

ocean floor

metamorphic rock

igneous rock

magma

Igneous rocks form in chains of volcanos above the ocean trenches. Once on the surface of the earth, these rocks are attacked by water, wind, and ice that break them into small pieces of sediment. These sediments are carried by rivers and streams, by desert winds, and by mountain ice, and they accumulate to form sedimentary rocks at the edges of continents and in the oceans.

New ocean crust appears at the bottom of the sea and disappears into the mantle again. When two continents, such as India and Asia, meet above a trench, they collide to form high mountains.

The sedimentary and igneous rocks of the continents are transformed by heat, pressure, and the enormous forces of the collision into the metamorphic rocks that make up the mountains. Eventually, the mountains are worn away and the sediment carried to the sea to begin the journey again.

The rocks which make up the crust of our earth have repeated these cycles for about four billion years.

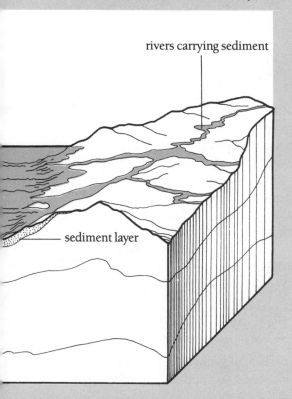

rivers carrying sediment

sediment layer

CHAPTER 4

Starting Your Rock Hunt

The author examines the folding of metamorphic rocks in Delaware.

How do collectors become interested in rocks and minerals? For some, it begins on a visit to the seashore or mountains. There are many places where you can collect rocks and minerals: in parks, fields, and woods, along the banks of streams, or on the shores of lakes or the ocean.

Here are some tips to make your collecting trips successful, and to help you identify your finds.

Smart Collecting

It's best to go collecting with a friend whenever you can, because it's fun to

42

share your discoveries. While you're just beginning your collection, you can probably find good specimens close to home. Later, you can plan trips further afield.

Building a first-rate collection takes time. Be careful – it's easy to catch "collector's fever": suddenly, it seems that the most important thing in the world is to find specimens, and you may start to pick up every rock in sight. Collecting is exciting, but remember that you have to lug home whatever you collect. Take only the best pieces, and leave some time to sort through the day's treasure.

Before you take any rocks from privately owned land, or from local, state, or national parks, you'll need to ask permission. In a park, go to the park office or ranger station and speak with someone in charge. You can also phone ahead for permission before you set out. (Look up Parks and Recreation in the city or county section of your phone book.) If you want to enter private property, ask the owner for permission. Most of the time, the owner will be happy to say yes, and will be pleased with your courtesy. This guarantees that you'll be able to make trouble-free return visits.

If you visit a building site, a quarry, or a mine, ask the supervisor for per-mission to collect rocks. It's very important to let the supervisor know when you are on the premises, and to follow his or her instructions exactly, because dynamite blasting or other dangerous work may be scheduled. Never go inside an abandoned quarry or mine. These usually have dump piles outside the entrances which contain good specimens and are more accessible (and much safer). Be careful around cables, wires, and equipment; stay away from areas marked hazardous. Wear a hard hat around building sites, mines, and quarries. This is a federal regulation.

Never enter a cave.

The best way to gather good rocks (and good information) is to go with a group of experienced collectors. You'll learn more about prime places to collect and you'll find better specimens if you work with an organized group.

Minerals and rocks have become so popular that there are more shops, clubs, and shows than ever. These can be valuable sources of information.

You can find rock shops by looking in your telephone directory. While you're at it, check out local science and hobby stores, too.

Try to find a local mineral or fossil club. Collecting with a club will give you access to the best sites in your area, many of which may be closed to individuals. Clubs may be listed in the phone book under a city or town name, or under "mineral," "fossil," or "rock." If there are no listings in the phone book, ask a local science teacher. Is there a park, natural history museum, or college with a geology department in your area? Someone there may know of a collecting club.

Each state in the U. S. has its own geological survey, which should be listed in the government section of your phone book under Department of the Interior. Canada's Geological Survey has provincial offices. The Survey is a good source for all kinds of geological information.

Mineral shows are held all over North America throughout the year; chances are there's at least one near you. Information on these shows is available at most rock and hobby shops and through collecting clubs and museums. These shows give you an opportunity to meet people who share your hobby, and you'll see some of the finest rock and mineral specimens in the world.

Collecting is great fun if you use common sense and take a few precautions. Have a great time!

Equipment

You don't need much equipment to start collecting rocks and minerals, and you can probably start today, using equipment found around the house. The basics include:

- a backpack to store your bounty
- a pair of work gloves or gardening gloves
- an 8X or 10X hand lens
- an old toothbrush and a few small paintbrushes (handy for dusting off delicate crystals and fossils)
- a strainer or small wire screen (to help separate large specimens from gravel)
- newspapers, toilet paper, and plastic bags to wrap your specimens
- small boxes, pill containers, or film canisters to store small, delicate rocks or crystals
- a first-aid kit with bandages and antiseptic
- a notebook, pen, and masking tape to help you keep track of your collection

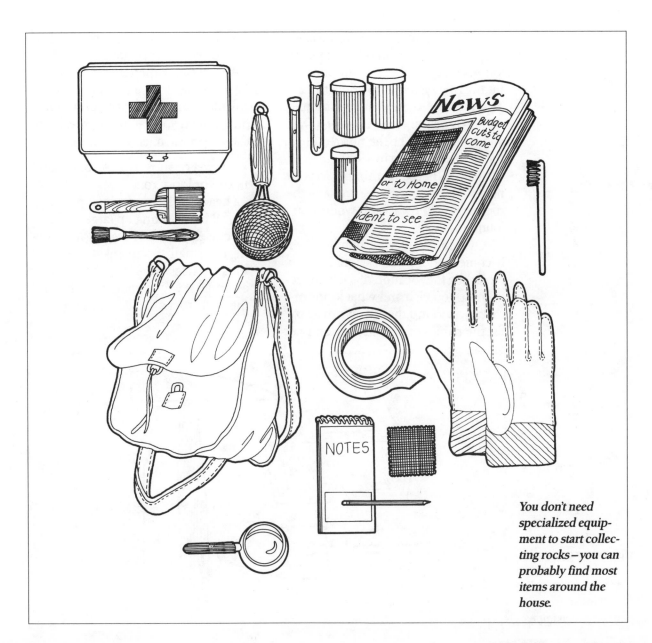

You don't need specialized equipment to start collecting rocks – you can probably find most items around the house.

When you find a rock you wish to keep, put a piece of masking tape on it and give it a number. A common numbering system is to add a three-digit number to the year you found the rock. For example, 89–001, 89–002, and 89–003 will be the first three rocks you collected in 1989.

Record that same number in your notebook along with the name of the rock (if you know it) and where you found it.

Over the years, your notebook will become a prized possession. Besides recording the location of each collection site you visit and what kinds of rocks you found there, you can also list the names of people to ask for permission, draw a simple map of each site, and record interesting incidents.

As you gain experience, you may wish to bring along a number of tools, available at most hardware or hobby stores, which you can use to break up rocks or pry them apart:

- a trowel or shovel, good for digging in soil or loose rock
- a heavy mallet and a rock pick, useful for breaking up large rocks
- a chisel, useful for digging and prying out small specimens
- plastic safety goggles – absolutely essential if you're going to be breaking apart rocks.

These tools are useful for digging up and breaking rocks. Always wear goggles when using the hammer.

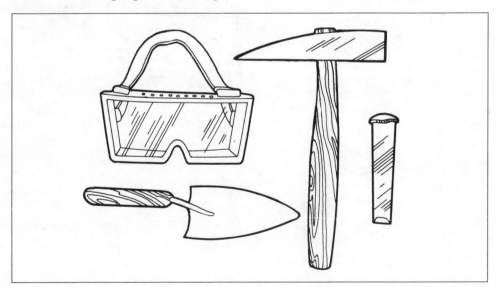

Standard carpentry hammers are not good substitutes for heavy mallets or rock picks. They're not made for hitting rocks, and they break easily.

Be extra careful when you hit rocks with any tool; keep your fingers and toes out of the way, and protect yourself from flying rock chips. It isn't necessary to hit the rock very hard; you'll have more control if you chip away at it rather than smashing it with a hammer. Warn others to stand clear before you start hammering, and keep your distance from anyone who is using a hammer.

Eventually, you may wish to explore unfamiliar areas in search of specimens. Learn to use a compass if you plan to explore uninhabited areas. Maps and guidebooks, available from rock shops and rock and mineral clubs, can help you find unusual collecting sites. In parts of Colorado and other areas, you may want to purchase pans and sieves to pan for gold in stream beds.

Always tell someone where you're going and when you expect to be back. If you plan to be out for a long time, be sure to bring a plastic bottle of drinking water.

Once you get your specimens home, they may need some cleaning. Soapy water and an old toothbrush may be all that's needed, but you may need to soak them in chlorine bleach for about 10 minutes to remove some stains or fungus. Be careful not to splash or spill the bleach, or to get any on your hands. Be sure to rinse off all traces of the bleach.

To clean delicate rocks or crystals, use a soft watercolor paintbrush, with or without water. Dental tools are excellent for cleaning the crevices of fossils. Ask your dentist to save old tools for you. Be sure to clean them in boiling water before using them (and watch out for those sharp points).

What Have You Found?

The kinds of rocks and minerals you find will depend upon where you look. If you pick up stones during a walk through the woods or along a beach, you'll see any number of different stones.

Identifying stones takes some detective work, but there are many

A stream carrying sediments smooths the sharp edges of the rocks it tumbles over.

clues. Often, knowing where a stone comes from is the first step in determining its history.

If a stone is smooth and rounded, chances are that it has spent a long time in a stream or river, or along a shore, where water and sand could wear away its rough edges. The stone probably came from far away and was carried by water.

A rough and jagged stone with an irregular shape may have been broken from a larger stone nearby, or it may have traveled hundreds of miles, frozen in the ice of an ancient glacier.

Rock or Mineral?

How can you tell if the stone you hold in your hand is a rock or a mineral? A rock is made of one or more minerals. If you can see pieces or grains of several colors in a stone, then you're looking at a rock. Don't be fooled by discoloration caused by dirt, staining by iron-bearing minerals, or by weathering. (Weathering, the natural process that breaks down minerals exposed to air and water, makes minerals look drab.)

If a specimen contains fossils, that's positive proof that it's a rock.

If your specimen seems to be made of only one material and is a solid color throughout, it may be a single mineral or it may be a rock containing individual minerals too small to see. The best way to decide whether it's a fine-grained rock or a mineral is to look for a broken edge (or break the specimen yourself with a hammer or pick). Rocks break in a more jagged, haphazard way than minerals. The next two chapters describe other ways you can identify rocks and minerals.

CHAPTER 5

Recognizing Minerals

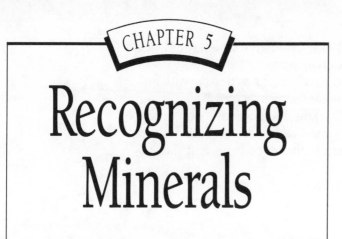

"Desert roses" are clusters of crystals formed by the evaporation of temporary lakes in the desert. This desert rose is made of gypsum.

Once you've found a mineral, the next step is to determine which mineral it is. Every mineral has its own set of features that can help you identify it.

LUSTER

The way a mineral's surface reflects light is described as luster. This is your first clue to identifying a mineral.

Does the mineral look shiny or dull? Most crystals have a shiny luster; metals have a metallic luster. Other types of luster are dull or earthy, greasy, and pearly.

COLOR

You might think that color would help you identify a mineral. It's probably the most eye-catching feature. But most minerals can be found in a variety of colors caused by small amounts of impurities. Still, looking at the color can be helpful. For minerals with a metallic or earthy luster, the color of the powdered mineral tells us more about the mineral's identity than the color of the whole specimen. But how do you powder a stone?

You make a streak. To do this,

you'll need a small piece of white, unglazed porcelain, which geologists call a *streak plate*. The back of a porcelain tile will do just as well as the streak plates sold in rock shops.

To make a streak, just rub the specimen across the tile. It will leave behind a line of powdered mineral. If you can't see a line, then the mineral has a white streak, or it may be harder than the porcelain, and leave no streak. Most minerals with shiny, non-metallic luster, such as quartz, have a white streak, but minerals with metallic or earthy luster usually leave streaks of black, green, brown, or red, which help identify them.

When your streak plate gets dirty, you can clean it with cleanser.

HARDNESS

Minerals also can be identified by their hardness, or their resistance to scratching.

Friedrich Mohs, a 19th-century German mineralogist, made a scale that shows the hardness of each mineral relative to other minerals. This is now called the Mohs scale of hardness. Mohs assigned a hardness of 1 to the softest mineral, talc, and a value of 10 to the hardest mineral, diamond. Diamond will scratch any

other mineral, and most minerals will scratch talc. The full scale, from 1 to 10, is shown here.

Hardness	Mineral
1	talc
2	gypsum
3	calcite
4	fluorite
5	apatite
6	feldspar
7	quartz
8	topaz
9	corundum
10	diamond

Your fingernail has a hardness of 2½ and will scratch both talc and gypsum.

A copper penny has a hardness of 3, just like calcite. If you carry a penny and a piece of quartz on collecting trips, you can identify minerals with hardness of less than 3, between 3 and 7, and greater than 7. This information, along with other information about color and other properties, is enough to distinguish among many minerals.

Many rock shops and natural history museums sell hardness kits. These contain a piece of all the minerals on the Mohs scale, except diamond. You can judge the hardness of any mineral you collect by scratching it with each mineral in a hardness kit.

CLEAVAGE AND FRACTURE

All minerals will break if you hit them hard enough. Some minerals break along certain planes, forming smooth, flat, shiny surfaces. These are called cleavage planes or cleavages. Many minerals have cleavage because their structure is weaker in some directions than in others. Mica can be split into thin, paper-like sheets along its one perfect cleavage plane. Other minerals break into cubes or rhombs, which look like boxes tilted to one side. A mineral can have as many as four cleavage planes.

A cleavage plane looks like the face of a crystal, but it is not the same. There will usually be more than one parallel surface for each direction of cleavage, because the mineral always breaks most easily in this direction. Crystals, on the other hand, form as the mineral grows larger. The shape of a crystal has nothing to do with how it breaks, and one crystal face may not be parallel to any other face.

Some minerals have no consistent patterns of weakness in their structures and do not break along cleavage planes. Instead, they break in a more irregular way, called fracture. Quartz is the most important and common mineral that shows fracture instead of cleavage. If you look at the fracture surfaces of quartz, you can sometimes see fine grooves forming a semicircular pattern that looks a little like a seashell. This is called *conchoidal fracture* (after the Greek word for shell) and it is a distinctive property of quartz.

Many native metals and minerals with metallic luster, such as magnetite and hematite, break in a jagged, uneven way called *hackly fracture*.

UNIQUE PROPERTIES

Some minerals have unusual qualities that distinguish them from all others. Magnetite, for example, is magnetic; a pocket magnet will stick to it. No other mineral is as magnetic as magnetite.

Quartz has a property called piezo-electricity. If you apply pressure to a quartz crystal, it produces a tiny electric current, too weak to be noticed without the proper equipment. If an electric current is applied to a thin slice of quartz, the mineral will vibrate at a rapid, steady rate. This property of quartz makes it useful in watches.

Some minerals are unusually heavy or unusually light. You can test minerals and rocks just by hefting them in your hand. Most minerals with metallic luster are heavier than other minerals because they contain such relatively heavy elements as iron. Graphite, however, is very light for a mineral with a metallic luster. It's made of the element carbon, which is much lighter than most elements.

Some minerals react when a few drops of mild acid, such as vinegar, touches them. The most common mineral with this property is calcite. A drop of vinegar will make calcite fizz and bubble. Slightly stronger acid will create more vigorous fizzing. The acid attacks the mineral and releases carbon and oxygen from within the crystal structure in the form of carbon dioxide gas (the same gas that makes bubbles in soft drinks). After you try this experiment, be sure to wash the specimen to remove the vinegar.

A Russian craftsman made this ornate case in the 1600s or 1700s to house a lodestone. Lodestones were used to magnetize iron for compass needles.

Your Field Guide to Common Minerals

Some minerals are easier to find than others, and their availability varies from place to place. This basic field guide will help you identify those specimens you're most likely to find during your rock-hunting trips.

Many more common and uncommon minerals that you may find are described in the field guides listed in "For More Information," page 119.

Cleavage in one direction

CALCITE

Luster: shiny
Color: usually white or colorless; may be beige to yellow, pink to red, gray, blue, or green
Streak: white
Hardness: 3
Cleavage/Fracture: three directions of cleavage; pieces bounded by cleavage planes form rhombs
Other: fizzes in vinegar

Calcite is a common mineral, often found in sedimentary rocks. Some marine animals make their shells from calcite produced by their bodies.

Limestone, the raw material of cement, is a rock made up mostly of calcite or dolomite (see "Dolomite" below). Calcite is also the main consti-

Calcite

tuent of marble, a metamorphic rock. Natural chalk contains calcite in a very fine-grained, almost powdery form.

Rhombs of calcite are often found as larger pieces break apart along cleavage planes. Calcite crystals have been found in more than 300 different shapes.

Calcite is usually found in caves, where it forms stalactites and stalagmites as it crystallizes out of water solutions. Hot springs and cold springs form calcite deposits called travertine or tufa; those at Mammoth Hot Springs in Yellowstone National Park in Wyoming are spectacular. Onyx marble, sometimes called Mexican onyx because much of it comes from Mexico, is made of banded calcite.

A colorless, transparent variety of calcite, called Iceland spar after its country of origin, can make a single image appear double when seen through the transparent crystal. This makes Iceland spar useful for many optical instruments.

DOLOMITE

Luster: shiny or pearly

Color: usually white, beige, or pink; may be gray, green, brown, or black
Streak: white
Hardness: 3 ½ to 4
Cleavage/Fracture: three directions of cleavage; pieces bounded by cleavage planes make rhombs
Other: fizzes slightly or not at all in vinegar

Dolomite is a common mineral found in many sedimentary rocks, such as limestones (called dolostones when dolomite is the most abundant mineral). Dolomite is a little harder than calcite and doesn't react as strongly to vinegar.

FELDSPAR

Luster: shiny
Color: mostly opaque and white; may be beige, pink to red, light to dark gray, green
Streak: white or none
Hardness: 6
Cleavage/Fracture: two directions of cleavage; adjacent cleavage planes meet at right angles.
Other: may look like quartz, but has cleavage instead of fracture.

Feldspar is actually a group of related minerals. They are the most abundant minerals within the earth's crust, but they quickly weather to clay, and so are not as common on the surface as quartz.

Feldspar is usually found in igneous rocks, where it may form small, perfect crystals. Feldspar forms the largest known crystals: a mass found in the Soviet Union weighed more than 2,000 tons.

A brilliant green to blue-green variety is called amazonstone. Moonstone is a milky feldspar with an opal-like quality. Sunstone has tiny flakes of hematite that give the feldspar a red color and a golden shimmer. Porcelain and other ceramics are made of feldspar.

FLUORITE

Luster: shiny or dull
Color: usually transparent; may be purple, green, blue-green, yellow, or colorless
Streak: white
Hardness: 4
Cleavage/Fracture: four directions of cleavage
Other: some varieties are fluorescent

Fluorite is common in sedimentary rocks, where it usually forms by hydrothermal action.

Fluorite crystals always form

Cleavage in two directions

Feldspar

cubes; beautiful, large crystals can sometimes be found lining cracks and cavities of rocks.

GARNET

Luster: shiny
Color: transparent to opaque and almost always deep red, purple-red, or brown-red; rare varieties are yellow, white, or green
Streak: white
Hardness: 6½ to 7½
Cleavage/Fracture: hackly fracture

Garnet, a group of closely related minerals, is one of the most common minerals in metamorphic rocks. It often forms crystals with 12 or 24 sides that resemble little faceted balls. Tiny red grains of garnet are often found in beach sand.

Transparent garnet is a common gemstone. The most prized variety, called demantoid, is green with a brilliant luster. It comes from the Ural Mountains in the Soviet Union. At Gore Mountain in New York's Adirondack region, a deposit of metamorphic rocks contains huge garnets–some individual masses as big as a room. These garnets have many fractures and are pulverized to make garnet sandpaper.

Garnets can be cut into faceted gemstones (top). They're often found within rocks, occasionally growing alongside other crystals. The sparkling crystals in the middle of the rock shown here are garnet. (The large crystal at far right is tourmaline.)

GRAPHITE

Luster: metallic or dull; sometimes looks greasy

Color: opaque, gray to silvery-gray or black

Streak: black

Hardness: 1 to 2

Cleavage/Fracture: one good cleavage direction, but cannot be peeled into sheets like mica; hackly fracture on other surfaces

Other: feels greasy; marks paper like a pencil

Graphite is most common in metamorphic rocks, but it also forms by hydrothermal action. Like a diamond, it's made of pure carbon, the basic element in all living things. Graphite probably was formed by the heating and pressurization of decayed plants and animals in sedimentary rocks. Today, nearly all graphite used in the United States is manufactured by heating coal in furnaces. Graphite also has been found in meteorites.

Graphite powder is used as a lubricant, and mixed with clay to make the "lead" in pencils.

GYPSUM

Luster: shiny or pearly

Color: usually colorless, white, or gray; may be yellow, red, or brown if impure

Streak: white

Hardness: between 2 and 2½

Cleavage/Fracture: one cleavage plane; hackly or conchoidal fractures on other surfaces

Cleavage in three directions

Gypsum, common in sedimentary rocks, may form transparent, colorless crystals that look like flattened rhombs. A fibrous variety forms veins called satin spar.

Fine-grained, white gypsum is used as the building stone called alabaster. Most gypsum is used to make plaster and fertilizers.

HALITE

Luster: shiny or dull

Color: usually colorless or white; may be yellow, red, blue, or purple if impure

Streak: white

Hardness: 2½

Cleavage/Fracture: three directions of cleavage; pieces bounded by cleavage planes form cubes

Other: dissolves easily in water

Gypsum

Halite is rock salt. It's found in many sedimentary rocks, and forms cube-shaped crystals.

Halite, or rock salt

Not all minerals are found in their crystal forms. Hematite, an important ore of iron, can form many shapes.

Mica

HEMATITE

Luster: metallic or dull
Color: usually opaque and reddish-brown or red; sometimes black and very shiny
Streak: light to dark red
Hardness: 5½ to 6½
Cleavage/Fracture: hackly fracture

Hematite is the most important iron ore. Small amounts of hematite are very common in many kinds of rocks.
This mineral gives some sedimentary rocks a red color. Shiny, black hematite may look like another mineral, such as magnetite, but its red streak always reveals its true identity.
Brown, earthy, iron-bearing minerals with a yellow-brown streak are related to hematite and are given the general name limonite.

MAGNETITE

Luster: metallic
Color: opaque and black, like iron
Streak: black
Hardness: 6
Cleavage/Fracture: hackly fracture
Other: naturally magnetic

Magnetite is usually present in very small amounts in all kinds of rocks. Some igneous and some ancient sedimentary rocks are made of almost pure magnetite, and are important iron ores. Its crystals have 8 or 12 sides.
No other mineral is as magnetic as magnetite.

MICA

Luster: shiny or pearly; may seem to have a metallic luster because of its silvery color
Color: colorless to silvery; light to dark brown, black; pink to purple
Streak: white
Hardness: 2 to 3
Cleavage/Fracture: one perfect

cleavage plane; thin sheets can be peeled off along this plane

Mica is the name for a group of minerals that are distinguished from each other by their color. Muscovite is colorless to silvery; biotite is brown to black. Chlorite is a related mineral that looks like green mica.

Mica is found in igneous and metamorphic rocks. Crystals of mica are six-sided. The largest specimens are called mica books.

The muscovite variety of mica is used for electrical insulation. In the 19th century, sheets of transparent colorless mica, called isinglass, were used as windowpanes.

PYRITE

Luster: metallic
Color: opaque and pale, brassy yellow
Streak: greenish-black or brownish-black
Hardness: 6 to 6½
Cleavage/Fracture: hackly or conchoidal fracture

Pyrite is the most common mineral with metallic luster. It's found in igneous, sedimentary, and metamorphic rocks, but it usually forms by hydrothermal action. It's often found

as cubes or many-sided crystals.

Pyrite was often mistaken for gold by inexperienced prospectors, earning it the nickname "fool's gold." Genuine gold has a more golden, less brassy color and is heavier. Gold, with a hardness of only 2 ½ to 3, is also much softer than pyrite.

Pyrite contains sulfur and is used to make sulfuric acid. Crystals or cut pieces of pyrite are sometimes used as jewelry.

Small crystals of pyrite, or "fool's gold," can be found in many kinds of rocks, in all parts of the country.

PYROXENE AND AMPHIBOLE

Luster: shiny
Color: usually opaque and black; some varieties are opaque and light to dark green, dark blue, or brown; others are transparent to opaque and colorless
Streak: white
Hardness: 5 to 6
Cleavage/Fracture: two perfect cleavage planes; hackly fracture along other surfaces

Its hardness and its attractive colors have made jade popular among master carvers for thousands of years. Jade can be found in white and in shades of green, rose, and pale blue.

Pyroxene and amphibole are two groups of related minerals found in igneous and metamorphic rocks. Sedimentary rocks rarely contain these minerals.

Most igneous rocks contain small black grains or crystals. If they are dull-looking and hard, they are pyroxene or amphibole. (If they are very shiny, soft, and can be peeled with your fingernail, they are mica.) If you look carefully with a magnifying lens, you may be able to see two shiny cleavage planes in the grains. Pyroxene and amphibole sometimes form crystals in igneous rocks. These look like columns with blunt ends; amphibole crystals are often longer and less stubby than pyroxene.

Within the pyroxene group are the minerals augite, diopside, jadeite, and bronzite. Some of the minerals in the amphibole group are hornblende, tremolite, actinolite, and nephrite.

Metamorphic rocks also may contain varieties of pyroxene and amphibole that are black, colorless, deep blue, or green. Jadeite and nephrite, commonly called jade, are examples of metamorphic pyroxene and amphibole.

Some asbestos minerals are fibrous amphiboles. The gemstone called tiger's eye is made of fibrous amphibole replaced by quartz.

QUARTZ

Luster: shiny
Color: crystals may be almost any color; white (milky quartz), pale pink (rose quartz), purple (amethyst), yellow (citrine), dark gray to black (smoky quartz),

other shades of green, red, brown, and blue; can also be colorless. Opaque varieties can be red (carnelian), brown (sard), apple green (chrysoprase), green with red spots (heliotrope or bloodstone), and banded.

Streak: white or none

Hardness: 7

Cleavage/Fracture: conchoidal fracture

Other: crystals are usually six-sided with one or two pointed ends

The most common mineral on the surface of the earth, quartz exhibits almost unbelievable variety. All quartz is made of silicon and oxygen. You may find clusters of quartz crystals lining a crack in a rock or filling the cavity of a geode. Individual quartz crystals weighing hundreds of pounds have been found. Colorless quartz and amethyst form the best crystals. Milky quartz and rose quartz seldom form good crystal shapes. Aventurine, a green variety of quartz, gets its color from flakes of the mineral chlorite.

Quartz is a common component of most rocks, usually as small, shapeless grains. Sandstone, for example, may be made mostly of rounded quartz grains.

Opaque quartz, generally called

You can find quartz in many different colors and shapes throughout the world. Crystals like these are worth hunting for.

chalcedony, is made of microscopic grains of quartz. Flint and chert are two varieties of chalcedony. They can be dark gray, brown, or black. Jasper is a yellow or red chalcedony.

Agate, a stone very popular as jewelry, has colorful layers that form as the agate crystallizes out of water along cracks or cavities in rocks. When the agate encloses spiky crystals of manganese oxide as it grows, moss agate results.

Onyx is a variety of agate with parallel layers of color. Brilliant red or blue agate is usually produced by dyeing.

Opal is a fiery, translucent variety of quartz.

Quartz sometimes replaces other minerals or decaying plants and animals. When wood cells are replaced by quartz, the result is petrified wood.

Since quartz is so abundant and can be found in so many varieties, you'll probably collect many kinds.

Agate

CHAPTER 6

Identifying Rocks

These blocks of granite in Yosemite, California, have been broken and moved by the actions of freezing and thawing.

Most rocks are easy to identify if the minerals they're made of are large enough to recognize. If a rock is very fine-grained, it's much harder to identify, but it can be done. Here's how.

The first thing is to find out whether the rock is sedimentary, metamorphic, or igneous. Sedimentary rocks are softer than metamorphic or igneous rocks. If you hit a sedimentary rock with a hammer, it will make a dull thud; metamorphic and igneous rocks, being harder, will ring when struck.

This test, plus careful observation, will help you identify all the rocks you collect.

Common Sedimentary Rocks

You can recognize sedimentary rocks by their layers. These layers, each a different color, are made by many kinds of sediments built up over time.

When these rocks were forming, plants or animals may have been buried in the sediments and become fossils. Shells, leaves, bones, and teeth all form common fossils. A stone that contains any of these is a sedimentary rock.

Rocks with large holes or crystals of quartz, calcite, dolomite, or fluorite are nearly always sedimentary rocks. Halite (rock salt) is found only in sedimentary rocks.

Sedimentary rocks are described by the material they contain. For example, if you find some sandstone with many fossils in it, you can call it "fossiliferous sandstone."

COAL

Even though it's made from the remains of plants, coal is considered a rock because heat and pressure have thoroughly changed the plants to a new form. It's considered to be sedimentary because it is usually found with other sedimentary rocks, especially shale.

The remains of plants that lived millions of years ago formed the coal we use today. This bituminous coal sample is from Wise County, West Virginia.

When pebbles are buried by sand that gradually turns to rock, the result is called conglomerate sandstone. This piece was found in Arizona.

This limestone shows sedimentary banding. Sometimes the bands become bent because limestone is soft and easily deformed.

Coal is black, lightweight, and has a shiny, almost waxy luster on some surfaces. Soft coal is called bituminous coal; hard coal, which has been subjected to greater heat and pressure, is called anthracite coal.

The best plant fossils are found in coal and in shale. Coal is one of our most important sources of fuel.

CONGLOMERATE

This is nothing more than gravel cemented together naturally into sedimentary rock. The gravel can be a mixture of any kind of minerals and pebbles. The cement can be made of quartz, calcite, or iron oxide.

Conglomerates are rarely used for building because they crumble easily, but small, well-cemented pieces can be cut and polished to make beautiful bookends and paperweights.

LIMESTONE

You may find deposits made of calcite, dolomite, or a combination of both. These minerals are described on pages 54 and 55.

Limestone may contain fossils of water-dwelling plants and animals. Limestone can be white, gray, black, or brown.

SANDSTONE

As its name suggests, this rock is made of sand grains cemented together. It feels gritty when you rub it with your fingers. Most sand contains a lot of quartz, so quartz is often the most abundant mineral in sandstone. The cement can be made of quartz, calcite, or iron oxide.

Sandstone is usually gray, brown, or red. It's a common building stone. Fossils are sometimes found in fine-grained varieties.

SHALE

This sedimentary rock is formed from silt and mud. It's very fine-grained, but usually has some layering or fossils that distinguish it from igneous and metamorphic rocks. It's also softer than those rocks.

Shale can be gray, brown, red, or black. It often contains fossils, including footprints of animals, or signs of natural processes, such as ripple marks.

Common Igneous Rocks

All igneous rocks were once hot (up to 2,000 °F), molten rock that solidified as it cooled.

Volcanic rocks, such as obsidian and basalt, form on the surface of the earth and cool faster than other igneous rocks. This quick cooling produces rocks with very fine mineral grains and prevents crystals from forming.

Most igneous rocks contain a mix of light-colored and dark-colored mineral grains. Fine-grained rocks with large crystals of feldspar, black pyroxene, or black amphibole are almost always igneous. Volcanic glass is always igneous.

These long, flowing ropes of lava, called pahoehoe (pa-HOY-hoy), were spewed from the Kilauea Volcano in Hawaii.

BASALT

This volcanic rock is black on its unweathered surfaces. It's very fine-grained, but sometimes has tiny green or white crystals. Basalt is not very common on land, but it's the most common rock on the ocean floor.

Basalt may be full of holes formed by escaping gas as the rock cooled. Crystals of quartz, calcite, and other minerals can grow in these holes, deposited by hot water circulating through the cooled rocks. Copper ore can be found among basalts in the upper peninsula of Michigan and other places. Red-brown basalt may look like clinker (see "Tuff and Pumice" below).

GABBRO

These igneous rocks form underground and are made almost entirely of feldspar and black pyroxene.

Like basalt, gabbros are usually very dark gray to black, but the mineral grains are visible.

GRANITE

Granite, the most common igneous rock on land, solidifies under the surface of the earth. You can recognize that granite isn't a volcanic rock

Granite is the most common igneous rock on the continents.

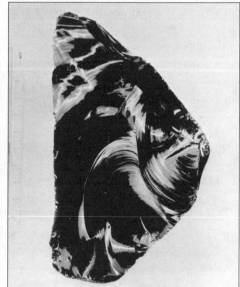

Obsidian looks like glass. It breaks along curved lines, and this kind of break is called a conchoidal fracture.

because you can easily see individual mineral grains.

Granite contains feldspar, quartz, and black pyroxene, amphibole, or mica. It's usually white, gray, pink, red, or beige; rare varieties are green, very dark gray, or black. Granite is one of the most popular building stones in the world.

OBSIDIAN

When molten lava cools so fast that mineral grains have no time to grow, it forms shiny volcanic glass called obsidian. Most obsidian is dark gray, black, or red. This smoky glass is so dark that you can't see through it, except for very thin pieces.

Obsidian may be more than one color if batches of molten rock were mixed when it formed. Sometimes you can find pieces with swirls of color that formed as the rock flowed like thick molasses. Look for conchoidal fractures on some surfaces.

Obsidian is often confused with

Tuff

slag, a waste material from smelting iron ore. Slag is often blue or green, which is rare for natural glass.

PORPHYRY

Sometimes, volcanic rocks contain good or even perfect crystals of feldspar, pyroxene, amphibole, or smoky quartz, up to an inch long. These crystals grow in the magma below the surface of the earth, and when the magma erupts and cools quickly, it forms fine-grained rock that surrounds the crystals.

These rocks are called volcanic porphyry. Porphyries can be almost any shade of gray, red, or brown, and sometimes green. Their crystals are usually white, gray, pink, red, or black.

TUFF AND PUMICE

When volcanos erupt, they spew ash that hardens into rocks called tuff or pumice. Pumice has more air bubbles than tuff and looks like a sponge. Both rocks are very light (pumice floats in water). They usually are white, gray, beige, or pale pink.

Cinder and clinker are synthetic materials from industrial furnaces that resemble tuff and pumice, but they are heavier and are usually dark red or brown. They are often used for fill.

Common Metamorphic Rocks

Metamorphic rocks were once igneous or sedimentary rocks. By heat and pressure inside the earth, they were transformed – or metamorphosed – into their present forms.

The minerals in most metamorphic rocks are arranged in one direction. Sometimes the grains are bent into kinks or folds. Rocks made almost entirely of amphibole or mica, and rocks with crystals of garnet, are almost certain to be metamorphic. Parallel grains of mica give metamorphic rocks very shiny surfaces, like no other kind of rock.

Sometimes gneiss has obvious stripes of color. The bands aren't so apparent in this sample, but the distinct mineral grains and the way the dark grains line up tell you that this is gneiss.

GNEISS

You can recognize gneisses by their bands of multicolored minerals. The individual mineral grains are visible. Feldspar and quartz are abundant in light gray or pink layers; mica, pyroxene, and amphibole are concentrated in layers of dark gray to black. Garnet also is common in gneisses.

Gneisses are rocks that have been intensely squeezed and metamorphosed. If heat and pressure are great enough, sedimentary rocks such as shale, as well as igneous rocks such as granite, can form gneisses.

MARBLE

When it is highly compressed and heated, limestone becomes marble. It may still look very much like limestone, but it contains larger mineral grains and is much harder.

The most abundant mineral in marble is calcite, but marble also can contain mica, garnet, green amphibole or pyroxene, quartz, feldspar, and small, shiny flakes of graphite. The graphite may be formed from the remains of plants and animals preserved

Can you identify the stones in your local buildings? The exterior of the Empire State Plaza in Albany, New York, is made of marble from Vermont and elsewhere; the State Capitol building on the far left is made of white granite from Maine; the egg-shaped Performing Arts Center is concrete, which is made with limestone.

in limestone and transformed by heat and pressure into pure carbon.

Marble has colorful patterns produced by layers of minerals that have been squeezed and folded during metamorphism. It's highly prized as building stone.

On the left side of this sample of slate, you can see how the rock chips off in flat layers; on the right side are veins of quartz.

QUARTZITE

This is metamorphosed sandstone. Most sandstone is made of quartz grains, so metamorphic sandstone is called quartzite. Quartzite can be white, gray, brown, or red.

Quartzite is sometimes confused with flint or other quartz rocks, but quartzite has larger grains. It is harder and holds together better than sandstone, and freshly broken quartzite feels smoother than sandstone, which feels bumpy or gritty.

SCHIST

Highly compressed and heated shale becomes schist. Schist is more coarse-grained than shale, and you can usually see individual minerals.

All schists contain silvery-white, black, or green mica compressed into parallel layers that reflect light. You may see folds in these layers. Garnet crystals often grow in schist.

SLATE

When shale is exposed to moderate heat and pressure, it becomes slate. Crystals of mica-like minerals start to grow during metamorphism, and are compressed into layers. Slate is easily split along these layers into thin slabs that are perfect for blackboards and shingles. The minerals in slate are still very small, however, and slate is as fine-grained as shale.

The best way to distinguish shale from slate is to tap it lightly with a hammer: slate "rings," while shale makes only a dull thud. Slate is usually red, green, or gray.

CHAPTER 7

Organizing Your Collection

There are so many varieties of rocks and minerals waiting to be collected that you may be surprised by how fast your collection grows. No one else will have quite the same rocks, so your collection can be a source of pride.

Some collectors hunt for certain kinds of rocks: some collect only crystals, some collect only fossils, and some might collect only colorful or oddly shaped rocks. Some people like to display the stones they find in their natural state; others like to polish them, carve them, or make them into jewelry.

When it comes to your collection, you're the boss. You may decide to do any of these things, or none of them.

Wherever you go, you'll find something new to add to your collection.

71

Storage and Display

To store a small collection of sturdy rocks and minerals, a shoe box or cigar box will do. You also can find clear plastic boxes, such as those made for sweaters or shoes, in variety and department stores.

Fragile crystals and fossils should be stored individually in small boxes, jars, or even in the individual compartments of an egg carton.

You may want to display your favorite specimens on a shelf while the

Design your rock display to fit the available space and the size of your collection.

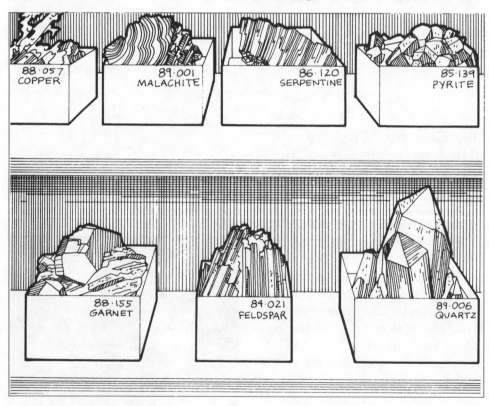

A simple note lets you keep track of where and when you found your samples.

rest of your collection is stored out of the way. You can change your display every few weeks, as your own private museum.

Some rocks look better wet. You can display these in an aquarium or a bowl of water, or you can shellac them.

It's a good idea to label each specimen. On a small card, write the specimen's name (if you know it), where you found it, and the date you found it. If you gave your rock a number when you collected it, write this number on the card. Keep the cards in a file, or display them next to each specimen.

If you wrote the number on a piece of masking tape and attached it to the rock when you found it, you can replace the masking tape with a more permanent label. Put a dab of white paint on an inconspicuous part of the sample. When the paint is dry, write the number on the rock with a fine-tipped, permanent pen.

Once your rocks and minerals are identified and labeled, how will you arrange them? It's entirely up to you.

You can arrange them according to whether they're igneous, sedimentary, or metamorphic; or alphabetically; or by hardness.

The hardest mineral in your collection will scratch all the others, but will remain unscratched. By using a piece of quartz (which you've probably already found), a penny, your fingernail, and the Mohs scale on page 51, you can estimate the hardness of all the minerals in your collection.

Crafts

Their shapes and colors make rocks ideal for sculpture and interesting free-form arrangements. You can arrange rocks into attractive patterns and glue them onto a cloth-covered board, or even make free-standing sculptures, bookends, or paperweights. White glue or craft cement works well for projects like these.

Rocking chairs? These Rock Settees by sculptor Scott Burton, carved of pink and green granite, are in the collection of the National Gallery of Art, Washington, D.C.

Certain rocks, such as soapstone, are soft enough to carve, although it takes training and a lot of care. Soapstone is made of very fine-grained talc and other minerals and is usually a pale green or pink color. It is found throughout North America. If you're interested in learning rock carving, visit a rock shop and ask a salesperson about it. (Sharp tools are needed, so be sure to learn about carving techniques and safety rules before you begin.)

Tumbling and Jewelry-Making

You can use any stone to make jewelry, but polished stones are more appealing than unpolished ones. You can find a selection of polished, precut stones at rock shops and gem and mineral shows, and you also can polish stones yourself by using a tumbler.

A tumbler is a closed container that is continuously rotated by a small motor. Unpolished stones are placed inside the container along with water and an abrasive powder called grit. As the container turns, the grit scrapes the stones, smoothing the rough edges and polishing the surfaces. Tumbled stones keep their individual shapes, but their surfaces become smooth and shiny. This doesn't happen overnight. To produce a good shine, the tumbler has to work for several days, and a series of different grits must be used, progressing from coarser to finer abrasives.

Most rock and hobby shops sell tumbling equipment and plans so that you can build your own tumbler.

Cabochons and faceted stones are

not produced by tumbling. They require more precise machinery, called lapidary equipment, which is very expensive and which is designed for professionals. Most lapidary equipment has motor-driven, rotating metal wheels with grit on their surfaces. These wheels grind stone surfaces into flat, polished facets. Several wheels must be used to achieve a progressively more brilliant polish. Some wheels have tiny diamonds embedded along their edges to cut the stones rather than grind them.

It's easy to make jewelry with tumbled or cut stones. Most rock and hobby shops sell link chains for necklaces and bracelets, metal holders and clamps for the stones, and clear hobby cement to secure the stones in their settings.

Most cut diamonds have 58 perfectly aligned facets. After it's cut, a diamond is polished against a revolving iron disk encrusted with diamond dust and coated with oil.

CHAPTER 8

Buried Treasure

The year is 1450. In a damp and dimly lit laboratory, an alchemist is hard at work. He is busy with a task that occupied his father, and his grandfather, and his great-grandfather. He is driven by a single goal shared by people for over 1,300 years – to find the formula that will turn common metals into gold.

Think of it! Imagine having the power to transform ordinary scraps of worthless metal into riches beyond belief!

Like thousands before him, the alchemist will devote his life to this quest. And, like those before him, he will fail.

The alchemist used his crude equipment for a noble purpose: to try to turn common metals into gold.

At your feet, locked inside rocks that are gray and green and even red, lie vast riches – gold, silver, copper, tin, and many other beautiful and useful metals. All these metals are minerals.

Sometimes, almost miraculously, certain metals can be found in their pure form – nuggets of gold, veins of silver, or other "native metals," formed underground in weird, tree-like shapes. More often, though, metals combine chemically with a variety of other elements to form ores. An ore is simply a rock or mineral from which metals may be extracted.

When metals combine chemically

77

When copper is found in its pure form, called native copper, the metal forms beautiful fern-like shapes (left). More often, copper combines with other elements as an ore, such as the green stone called malachite (below). Copper may be extracted from malachite, or malachite may be cut and polished as a gemstone.

with other elements, the result is often a substance that looks completely different from the elements that produced it. For example, when shiny copper combines with oxygen, an invisible gas, it forms the mineral cuprite, which has beautiful, dark red crystals; when it combines with oxygen and hydrogen (another invisible gas), it becomes the mineral malachite, which has bands of rich green and is often used to make jewelry. Copper also can combine with black iron and yellow sulfur to form brassy-yellow chalcopyrite.

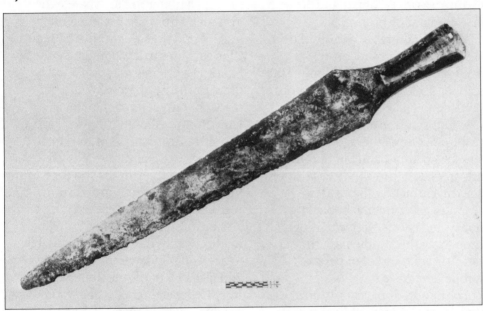

This primitive tool, an ancient copper spearhead, was unearthed in Houghton County, Michigan. Copper ore can still be found in this area.

Ore, Axes, and Autos

Copper has many uses—from pennies to electrical wiring—but it took thousands of years for people to learn how to separate copper from ore and to collect it in a form they could use. The answer was heat: the ore was melted in a brick furnace until the copper ran out. This is called smelting.

About 6,000 years ago, copper ore became the first material to be smelted. A thousand years later, a new and stronger material was created by melting copper with another metal, tin. When two or more metals are combined, the result is called an alloy. It was soon found that the strongest mixture was 90% copper and 10% tin. We call this alloy bronze.

Various cultures in the Middle East and China began using bronze at about the same time, from about 5,000 to about 2,500 years ago. Soon bronze was used to make weapons as well as vases, cups, and jewelry for the wealthy. But there was a problem: copper ore was abundant, but tin ore was rare, at least in the Middle East. To provide their armies with bronze weapons, governments pooled their money and efforts. Active trading throughout the Middle East, the Persian Gulf area, and even parts of Europe developed.

For hundreds of years, bronze was a metal reserved for soldiers and for the wealthy. It wasn't until someone discovered how to smelt iron that metal implements became available to everyone, even peasants.

Iron was used in some objects more than 5,000 years ago; iron beads have survived from ancient Egypt, and iron tools have been found in the Mediterranean region. But these were made not from iron ore, but from pure iron that was found in meteorites – and these were rare, indeed!

Iron ore is the most common ore on earth, but it must be smelted at even higher temperatures than copper or bronze. Someone had to find a way to build a hotter fire to separate the iron metal from the useless molten rock. Wood fires weren't hot enough. Charcoal fires worked much better. By building a brick furnace on a hill to draw air in, the charcoal could be made to burn at an even higher temperature. About 2,500 years ago, people in Armenia developed iron smelting. The techniques passed to a group called the Hittites and then to the Middle East and Europe. Iron materials were stronger than copper and bronze, and once they could be made cheaply, they became available to everyone. Today, to make steel, we add just a bit of the element carbon to iron. Other elements are also added to produce custom metals for just about any use.

In recent years, aluminum has begun to replace iron and steel because aluminum is much lighter and doesn't rust. Small amounts of other elements can be added to aluminum to make it stronger and more heat-resistant.

Aluminum ore is not like iron or other metal ores. The aluminum foil, soda cans, and other products we use so often come from an ore called bauxite that forms as a kind of soil in the southern United States and many other parts of the world. When water and vegetation have removed all other elements from the soil, bauxite is left behind. Bauxite ore must undergo a complex chemical process that consumes a lot of electricity to turn it into 99% pure aluminum metal. The result is worth it: planes, trains, automobiles, building materials, engine parts, appliances, pots and pans, and spacecraft all contain aluminum.

Because aluminum is costly to produce, products are often recycled; this helps to conserve electricity as well as the world's supply of bauxite. So the soft drink cans you take to the recycling center could become part of the next space shuttle.

Gold–The Perfect Metal

One metal is prized above all: gold. For thousands of years, gold has been regarded as the one perfect metal. Maybe this is because gold is rare; maybe it is because virtually all gold exists in its pure state, as native metal, not combined with other elements except a small amount of silver. Maybe its glorious color makes it our most coveted metal. Whatever the reasons, whenever people want to establish the value of something, including the worth of entire countries, they do so by using gold.

Gold has played a major role in the growth of knowledge through the early practice of alchemy. Alchemy began

It never tarnishes, won't rust, and can be hammered into thin sheets. It's gold, the world's most precious metal.

Gold is almost always found in its pure form, most of it as grains or thin veins running through rocks. This sample is from Colorado.

in Egypt and China at the same time, about 100 years after the birth of Christ. Both cultures regarded gold as the perfect metal and tried to change other metals into gold. Although alchemists failed in their attempts to change one substance into another, their efforts led to the modern science of chemistry.

For mystical philosophers who believed that life on earth is a reflection of events in the stars, the dream of transforming ordinary metal into gold was a symbol of the process of perfecting the human soul. Chinese philosophers sought a material which could be added to metals to turn them into gold. They called this mythical substance the Philosopher's Stone.

During the European Renaissance, between 1400 and 1500 A.D., wealthy patrons supported alchemists in hopes of increasing their stores of gold. It was not until the end of the 1700s that a new understanding of the chemical behavior of elements finally persuaded alchemists to give up their quest.

There is no way to change another metal into gold chemically; but we now know that it can be done only by changing the very nature of the atoms in a nuclear reaction. Still, it was the experiments of the alchemists that led to a deeper understanding of all the elements on earth.

Gold objects can be found in every culture. Here is an ancient gold figure from South America (top) and a modern royal dagger from the Middle East.

CHAPTER 9

Gemstones

In the fascinating forms and sparkling colors of minerals, we find an unending source of beauty and pleasure. Minerals in the form of gemstones have been admired and prized for about as long as we can imagine.

Napoleon gave this magnificent crown to his second wife, Marie Louise, in 1811. It has 950 diamonds and 79 turquoise cabochons.

What Makes a Mineral a Gem?

Almost any mineral can be considered a gemstone if it has certain qualities: beauty, durability, and rarity. The most important of these is beauty. Transparency, color, and sparkle all contribute to a stone's beauty.

People have always been drawn to the colors of gemstones – the rich red of rubies, the deep blue of sapphires, and the royal purple of amethysts. Emeralds are prized for their brilliant green color, even though they contain many tiny cracks that limit the transparency of the stones. In ancient cultures, color was often the only way to distinguish one mineral from another. The stone that was known as carbuncle was any one of the three red minerals which we know today as ruby, spinel, and garnet.

Gems are cut and polished to enhance their beauty and increase their value. The art of cutting stones began in southwestern Asia more than 6,000 years ago. Pictures of kings, religious figures, battles, and decorative patterns were etched into the surfaces of small gemstone cylinders called cylinder seals. These cylinders were rolled over the wax seals of documents, impressing the hot wax with the pictures on the seal. In this way, the authorship and authenticity of important documents was assured.

When stones were first used as decoration, they were cut into a smooth, domed shape called a *cabochon*. Today, transparent stones are usually cut and polished into many smooth, flat surfaces called facets, which increase the stones' brilliance by reflecting light. The most

Cameos are made of carved ivory attached to a dark cabochon-cut stone.

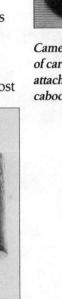

These stone cylinder seals from the Near East are about 4,000 years old.

common shapes are the round brilliant cut, the pear brilliant cut, the marquise cut, the square or table cut, the rose cut, and the emerald or step cut.

Valuable gems are durable; they are not easily scratched or broken. The most highly prized gemstones are in limited supply or their production is strictly controlled. If new sources of the gems are discovered and the supply of stones increases, the price of the gem will usually decrease. At the moment, emeralds are more rare than – and their price is comparable to – diamonds.

Egyptian emerald mines supplied the pharaohs almost 2,000 years ago, and are now open to tourists. The best source of these deep green stones today is Colombia. The mines are owned by the state and patrolled by armed guards, but many stones are smuggled out and sold illegally.

Scarcity is only one factor that affects the value of gemstones. The whims of fashion and superstition also have an impact. Opals, for example, are very fashionable today, yet during the nineteenth century, these stones were considered unlucky. Garnet, a favorite in Victorian times, has been out of vogue for many years.

Gemstones are also a convenient way to stash riches. A handful of perfectly cut stones can be worth as much as a wheelbarrow full of paper money. For centuries, gems have been used to hoard and transport wealth, concealed from enemies and governments.

Diamonds are the most important gemstones. High-quality diamonds are prized as jewelry; lower-quality

This fabulous diamond, in an equally striking setting, is called the Victoria Transvaal diamond.

diamonds and diamond dust are vital for industrial processes such as polishing, grinding, and drilling.

Diamonds form deeper than 100 miles beneath the earth's crust. Eruptions of magma and gases within the earth form channels called kimberlite pipes, through which rocks containing diamonds are propelled to the surface as fast as a jet plane. Diamonds are extremely durable. The rock surrounding a diamond can erode, and loose diamonds can be washed away or buried within newly forming rock.

Most early diamonds were found as loose stones in streams and rivers in India. Today, most diamonds come from mines in South Africa, the Soviet Union, and Australia. Diamonds have also been found in Arkansas.

Tourmaline is prized for its variations in color. It may have bands of white, pink, green, or black. Jewelry carved from pale pink and green tourmaline, called "watermelon tourmaline," is especially attractive.

Alexandrite (its mineral name is chrysoberyl) is a gem that has the unusual property of changing color in different kinds of light. It appears green in daylight, but changes to red in artificial, incandescent light – an emerald by day and a ruby by night. Alexandrite was discovered in the Ural

The world's largest cut gem is the Brazilian Princess, a 9½-pound topaz. Holding the gem is George Harlow, curator of minerals and gems at the American Museum of Natural History.

Mountains of Russia in 1830 and was named for Czar Alexander II. The Soviet Union is still the source of the most dramatic stones.

Jade is the popular name for two different minerals: jadeite and nephrite. Both minerals may be green,

This white jade perfume pendant shows how intricately this stone can be carved.

white, or gray. Although they can be carved, they are very tough and resist breakage.

Jade has long been highly valued by cultures throughout the world, including the Aztecs and Mayas in Central America and Mexico, the Maoris of New Zealand, and the Chinese. Jade was first used in China, where it reached its highest expression in exquisite carvings of emerald-green "imperial jade."

Ruby and sapphire are forms of the same mineral, corundum. Their colors are the result of small amounts of impurities in the gems. Rubies are red, less abundant, and more valuable than blue sapphires. Non-transparent star rubies and star sapphires contain tiny, needle-like crystals. When the stones are cut into a cabochon shape, a star pattern can be seen.

It's easy to see how the star sapphire earned its name.

The perfect crystals of quartz that grow in Herkimer County, New York, are called Herkimer diamonds.

Quartz, in all its many colors and varieties, is a significant but relatively inexpensive gemstone. Forms of quartz are found throughout the world. Besides forming beautiful gems, it has other properties that make it vital to technology.

Transparent varieties range from colorless to purple to black. Opaque quartz includes agate, with its bands of color, and opal, which has a unique internal structure.

Like ordinary quartz, opal is made of the elements silicon and oxygen, together known as silica. In opal, silicon and oxygen are joined as microscopic spheres. These silica spheres are so small that a human hair is 300 to 400 times thicker: you would need to place 100,000 of these spheres side by side to make a line one inch long. The spaces between the silica spheres are filled with air and water. Light that strikes an opal passes through the spaces in the structure and emerges as flashes of color. Opal is found throughout the world, but the best specimens come from Australia.

Magic Crystals?

Some people believe that gemstones have invisible powers that can help improve their lives. This idea is not new.

Centuries ago, crystal balls carved from clear quartz were used in many cultures in the Middle East, Asia, and Europe to try to forecast the future. In ancient civilizations, kings and warriors wore diamonds into battle because they believed that these exceptionally hard gems would make them invincible.

Once, gemstones had religious significance. The ceremonial breastplate worn by the high priest of the Twelve Tribes of Israel included stones called sardius, topaz, carbuncle, emerald, sapphire, diamond, agate, amethyst, beryl, onyx, jasper, and ligure. (Not all these names have meanings we recognize today; for example, ligure was probably the stone we call zircon.)

Later, astrologers assigned a gem to each of the twelve signs of the zodiac; these came to be called birthstones. Many people enjoy wearing a jewel that corresponds with the month of their birth.

Even though they can't foretell the future, these spheres, carved out of quartz crystal are bewitching.

BIRTHSTONES

January – garnet
February – amethyst
March – bloodstone or aquamarine
April – diamond
May – emerald
June – pearl, moonstone, or alexandrite
July – ruby
August – sardonyx or peridot
September – sapphire
October – opal or tourmaline
November – topaz or quartz
December – turquoise or zircon

Lab-Grown Gems

Synthetic minerals, including gemstones, now play an important role in industry and manufacturing. Most minerals created in the laboratory are made by melting a powder containing the elements needed to make the mineral, then cooling the molten mixture to let crystals grow. Synthetic rubies and sapphires, including star varieties, are grown in this way. Most stones produced by melting contain imperfections— bubbles and tiny scratches— that identify them as synthetic.

Another technique, called the hydrothermal growth process, grows crystals from hot water containing bits of the same mineral. Everything is enclosed in heavy steel containers under high pressure and at high temperature. Minerals are placed in the hot water at one end of the container, where they begin to dissolve. The steam carries the elements to the other end, where new crystals grow. This process mimics the natural growth of crystals underground in hot water that circulates among cracks in rocks. Quartz is the most common

mineral synthesized in this way. More than 700 tons of synthetic quartz is grown worldwide each year for industrial and commercial uses.

Some manufactured materials have the properties of minerals but are never found in nature: these are called synthetic minerals. YAG (yttrium aluminum garnet) is one of these substances. It has a structure identical to garnet but is made of elements not found in natural garnet. YAG is used as an industrial substitute for diamonds, and it also is used in some "ruby" lasers.

Lasers are very powerful, concentrated beams of light. Some lasers contain a crystal of ruby, synthetic ruby, or YAG. When an intense white light shines on these red crystals, they emit red light. This red light is bounced back and forth between two mirrors until a very concentrated beam of light is produced.

Ruby and YAG lasers are used in surgery to focus tiny, powerful beams that can safely cut in places where knives are too large to be used.

Gem Detectives

Gemstones are valuable and often hard to find, and it can be hard to tell the difference between an inferior stone and a perfect one, or even a synthetic stone from the real thing. A zircon can look like a diamond; synthetic rubies may be sold as natural rubies. Gemologists are trained to identify natural and synthetic gemstones.

The easiest way for gemologists to identify an unknown mineral is to grind it into a powder and analyze it with an kind of X-ray machine. Each mineral makes its own X-ray pattern, just like you have your own unique fingerprint. But the last thing anyone would want a gemologist to do is to grind a precious gem into a powder! Gemologists usually use other methods to identify a mineral. Each mineral has certain characteristics – hardness, heaviness, and optical properties. Equipment for evaluating gems ranges from a simple magnifying lens to powerful microscopes, and such complex tools as refractometers, spectroscopes, and X-ray diffractometers.

CHAPTER 10

From Stone Age to Space Age

Imagine that you're one of the first humans, living about 500,000 years ago. You've learned to use the stones around you as tools and weapons: sharp ones to cut plants; large, heavy ones to kill animals. One stone chips another to make a thin, sharp cutting edge. Two stones struck together make sparks that start fires for cooking and for warmth. Your survival depends on your use of the rocks around you.

Now imagine it's the future, not too far from today. A group of excited tourists has just lifted off on one of the space shuttle's routine tours of the upper atmosphere. But you're right here on earth – or, more accurately, just a few inches above it – on a super-fast, ultra-comfortable train that floats above magnetic rails as it speeds you toward your destination. You check your digital watch. It looks as if you're right on time.

A silicon chip the size of a dime may contain thousands of circuits. Such chips are the most important invention of this century, although their raw materials are as old as the earth.

Our earliest ancestors depended upon the stones they found around them. Today, we use rocks and minerals in much more sophisticated ways, but we continue to depend upon them.

Stone provides the material for the heat shields on the U.S. space shuttle. The potential of minerals as supercon-

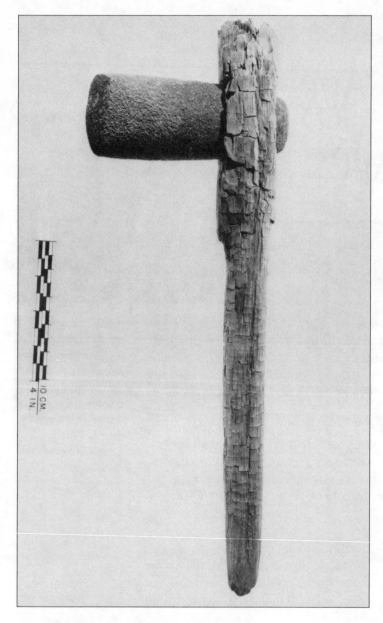

ductors is now being explored for electronics and transportation. Quartz crystals keep wristwatches accurate, and the synthetic ruby is the heart of powerful medical lasers.

The earliest stone tools were made more than two million years ago in East Africa by ancestors of humans. By about 50,000 years ago, humans made hooks, spearheads, and axheads of stone. One of the best rocks for making tools is flint, a common form of quartz that can be chipped into thin, sharp cutting edges, and which makes sparks when struck. Flint is found in deposits of clay or limestone. The purest deposits are found near the English Channel and in Belgium.

An ancient stone hatchet with a wooden handle, uncovered in Genessee County, Michigan.

Feats of Clay

Clay is a precious resource for the Taos Indians of Taos, New Mexico, who use it to make adobe to build their village.

About 10,000 years ago, humans began to take notice of one of the humblest materials of all, common clay. The tiny fragments of minerals and rocks that make up clay are so small that you would need a microscope or an X-ray machine to identify the individual fragments.

When clay is mixed with straw or grass, molded into bricks, and dried in the sun, it's called *adobe*. This was the first building material, used since prehistoric times. The Aztecs used adobe to build the Pyramid of the Sun in Teotihuacán, Mexico, five centuries ago – and it stands today. Adobe is still

Common clay has been used to make pottery for thousands of years. Shown here are a Minoan vase (top) and a Mexican funeral urn. A Greek jar, called an amphora, is pictured on page 97.

used in the southwestern United States, Mexico, and South America.

Thousands of years ago, someone thought to heat clay bricks in a fire, and the bricks became stronger. Clay baked at high heat is called ceramic. Egyptian builders used ceramic bricks about 7,000 years ago, and part of the 5,000-year-old Great Wall of China is made of ceramic bricks.

Early ceramics weren't limited to brickmaking. Ceramic pots and jars—pottery—were used to store water and food. Many tribes of Native Americans, especially those of the southwestern United States, made beautiful pottery with bold geometric designs. In China, pottery was considered an art form more than 1,000 years ago. Chinese artisans sculpted delicate objects from the fine, white clay called porcelain which is still used today.

Ceramics are probably more important than ever. Many fine-grained combinations of minerals are fired in furnaces to make modern ceramics. The magnets you may have on your refrigerator—ferrites—are magnetic ceramics containing iron. To make fuel for nuclear power plants, uranium is added to ceramic rods. Even a bulletproof vest contains some ceramic.

The tiles that cover the outside of the U.S. space shuttle are made of a ceramic strong enough to withstand the heat and shock of entering the earth's atmosphere. Scientists are creating brand-new ceramics called superconductors that conduct electricity exceptionally well when cooled to 350 °F below freezing. When electricity flows through these supercooled ceramics, a magnetic field develops that is powerful enough to actually hold them suspended in space. Ceramic superconductors that work at room temperature just might power the trains of the future.

A World of Silicon

The element silicon is nothing special to look at: it's a very dark gray, brittle solid with a metallic luster. Combined with oxygen, it forms quartz, the earth's most common mineral.

The same quartz that was chipped into flint arrowheads 50,000 years ago is a vital part of today's computers, solar cells, and high-speed communications systems.

Scientists combine silicon with such compounds as germanium,

This Greek amphora, used for carrying wine or oil, depicts a marriage procession.

From sand to circuitry, clockwise from left: All semiconductor chips are made mostly of pure silicon grains which are melted and shaped into thin wafers. The wafers are etched with the circuit pattern, cut, and fitted into protective cases, producing the integrated circuit.

gallium arsenide, cadmium sulfide, cadmium telluride, and lead telluride to make semiconductors. These devices regulate an electric current passing through them. Very small semiconductors are ideal for creating electronic circuits in such essential tools as hearing aids and computer chips.

Semiconductors in solar cells convert energy from sunlight into electricity. If we can learn how to make solar cells that are less expensive to produce and capable of storing more energy in less space, they may be the energy source of the future.

Silicon and silica glass are the basis of new telephone technology that lets people around the world communicate quickly and efficiently. Silica glass, also called fused quartz, is a very pure glass made by melting together silicon and oxygen and then cooling the mixture very quickly, before it can form crystals.

This new technology uses lasers and computers to convert the spoken word into signals of light. These laser beams of light are guided through ultra-thin strands of silica glass, called optical fibers. At the other end of the line the information is retranslated into speech by light-sensitive silicon semiconductors. With these new tools for communicating, we can send words and pictures to the other side of the globe almost at the speed of light.

Minerals are essential to this new type of laser-welding procedure. The laser light is produced by a crystal of a synthetic mineral called YAG; the light is aimed and focused by fiber-optic light guides made of silica glass, which is derived from common quartz.

CHAPTER 11

The Latest Word

A glacier scooped out the earth in Summit County, Utah, and formed Red Castle Lake.

Scientists love to argue. If you show a rock to ten geologists, they'll tell you ten different stories about how it formed.

Geology is an exciting area of study because new ideas are emerging all the time. Here are a few of the "hot topics" in geology today.

Life at the Bottom of the Sea

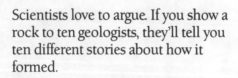

Geologists explore the continents and beyond. Since the 1960s, they've been diving to the bottoms of seas to study the ocean floor. How do scientists get to the bottom of the ocean? *Alvin*! *Alvin* is a small vessel called a submersible that can dive miles below the surface. *Alvin* and similar submer-

sibles are exploring the oceans all over the world, and also have been used to investigate the *Titanic* and other wrecks.

Recently, geologists have found rocks on the sea floor that explain how some ore deposits on land were formed – and they've discovered creatures that no one ever dreamed existed.

These discoveries have been made along the ocean ridges, chains of undersea volcanic mountains where new ocean floor is being formed. Capping some of these ridges are columns of rock, a few feet high, out of which pour boiling water and steam. These columns look like smokestacks, and geologists call them chimneys, vents, or black smokers. The steam is seawater heated to boiling as it circulates through cracks in basalt lava recently erupted on the sea floor. As the super-hot water meets the cold seawater, minerals that are dissolved in the hot water are deposited on the sea floor and form the chimneys. These chimneys are very rich in copper, iron, lead, and zinc ores.

Scientists recently located a field of such vents off the coast of southern Oregon. These 10-foot tall vents are spewing 500 °F water 10,000 feet below the surface of the sea.

These deposits on the sea floor help explain the origin of similar deposits of copper and other metals on land. One of the most famous copper ore deposits, on the Mediterranean island of Cyprus, was the major source of copper there thousands of years ago. Geologists now realize that the copper

Who knows what mysteries lie at the bottom of the sea? Alvin does! This Deep Submersible Vehicle (DSV) has made more than 2,000 dives in 25 years and showed us sights we couldn't begin to imagine. The 25-foot submersible accommodates three researchers.

A plume of hot, mineral-rich water spews from beneath the ocean floor through recently discovered volcanic vents.

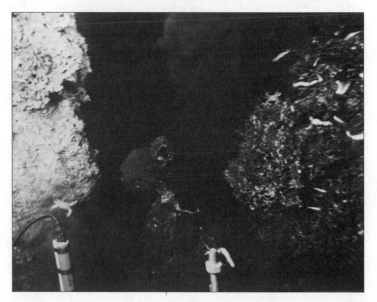

Exotic sea creatures, like this colony of giant worms, have recently been found thriving near underwater vents. These worms have bright red tips and live in 1-inch diameter tubes attached to rocks on the ocean floor.

ore on Cyprus first accumulated on the ocean floor millions of years ago. As the continents shifted, this part of ocean floor was pushed up onto the continent, becoming part of the island of Cyprus.

An even more surprising find was the recent discovery of "new" animals living around the chimneys, thousands of feet below the surface of the ocean, where sunlight never penetrates. These creatures include dark red worms up to 10 feet long and clams as large as dinner plates. Bacteria living inside these animals produce chemicals that nourish them.

Questions from Outer Space

Throughout our earth's history, there have been times when large numbers of creatures have died. Such a time is called a mass extinction. The most famous mass extinction happened about 66 million years ago, when all the dinosaurs and many other kinds of animals and plants disappeared.

What killed the dinosaurs? One possible answer comes from space.

A few years ago, a group of scien-tists discovered a high concentration of some unusual elements, including iridium, in 66-million-year-old clay. These elements are very rare on earth, but are common in meteorites. If an enormous meteorite struck the earth about 66 million years ago, it could have filled the atmosphere with dust, blotting out the sun and drastically cooling the planet. Green plants, which depend on the sun for energy,

Meteor Crater, Arizona, was created when a colossal meteor slammed into the earth about 50,000 years ago. The crater is more than 4,000 feet wide and 570 feet deep. Most of the meteorite was probably vaporized on impact.

would have died; then plant-eating animals would have starved, followed by the starvation of meat-eating animals. Some plants ultimately would have survived because seeds could stay dormant for several years and sprout later when conditions improved.

Some geologists think that mass extinctions have occurred on earth about every 30 million years. Astronomers have suggested that a disturbance of an area of dust and rocks at the far reaches of the solar system, called the Oort Cloud, may cause an unusual number of comets or meteors to collide with earth. The disturbance could be caused by the orbit of a tiny companion star that travels alongside our sun, or by the orbit of a tenth planet, "Planet X," between Neptune and Pluto. In either case, if the orbiting object crossed the Oort Cloud every 30 million years, it could produce meteorite bombardment of the earth and cause mass extinction. Like Planet X, the companion star may or may not exist, but the theory of its destructive power has earned it the nickname Nemesis, for the Greek goddess of vengeance.

Are these scientists correct? The evidence that an extraterrestrial object collided with the earth about 66 million years ago is convincing. But many geologists point out that dinosaurs and other creatures did not become extinct within a few years, as the impact theory might predict. Extinction occurred over a period of several million years. This points to a more complicated explanation for mass extinction.

Astronomers are searching for a Nemesis star or a Planet X in our solar system. If it is found—and if the theory is correct—we have about 25 million years to plan for the next meteorite and its consequences.

The Deep Freeze

We live during an ice age. It began about 2½ million years ago, when huge sheets of ice called glaciers advanced southward from the North Pole, covering parts of North America and Europe. During warmer periods, the glaciers shrank, only to expand again during cooler periods.

About 10,000 years ago, the glaciers retreated from North America and Europe to their present position around the North Pole. They left behind a record of their passing, gouging out the Great Lakes and depositing the sand and gravel that we use to make concrete and fill sandboxes. New England's clay and gravel industries owe their existence to glaciers.

In Antarctica and on Greenland, glacial ice can be 10,000 feet thick. Glaciers expand as snow falls on them and gradually becomes compacted

Glaciers moving along their slow but unstoppable paths carry dark bands of sediment and rock debris, and create this breathtaking marbleized effect when seen from the air. This photo shows the Malaspina Glacier, Alaska.

into ice. When the temperature rises and the ice melts, they shrink. Glaciers also can move under their own weight, sometimes gliding over a thin layer of water at their base.

Although the glaciers have retreated, they will advance again. Many scientists believe this will happen within 20,000 to 30,000 years, but the timing is hard to predict because air pollution is raising the temperature of our planet.

What Geologists Do

Geologists are scientists who study all parts of our planet, from its core to its surface. They also study meteorites and other objects in our solar system and other parts of the universe.

Geologists can specialize in many different features of the earth. Geologists who study fossils and ancient life are called paleontologists. Those who try to learn how igneous and metamorphic rocks form are called petrologists. Structural geologists look at squeezed and folded rocks and think about how plate tectonics affects large masses of rock. You can probably guess what mineralogists and sedimentologists study. Some geologists try to solve problems that overlap with

other sciences and so are called geochemists or geophysicists. And many geologists just call themselves "geologists"–the general practitioners of the earth.

Most geologists work for companies that supply coal, oil, and gas for energy; some work for companies that mine other earth materials – metal ore, building stone, clay, sand, or gravel. Geologists in all specialties work together to understand how deposits form so that they can get the material out of the ground most efficiently and find similar deposits in other places.

Paleontologists use microscopes to examine samples of sediment, looking for tiny fossils that signal a possible

Volcanos, earthquakes, and glaciers can change the face of the earth, but humans can create equally catastrophic results. This photograph is an aerial view of an open-pit copper mine in Pima County, Arizona, in 1978. Mines such as this can increase erosion and destroy plant and animal life. Most companies are required to restore the land after mining is completed.

This geologist, who works for a petroleum company, is collecting rocks and fossils, hoping to find evidence of an oil deposit.

petroleum deposit. Geophysicists study pictures of the earth's surface taken by orbiting satellites. Some geologists who supervise mining operations and the drilling of wells can create a picture of underground deposits in order to predict the next good place to mine or drill. Geologists also play an important role in protecting our environment. Many work for agencies of the federal government, such as the Environmental Protection Agency, or for private companies dedicated to cleaning up our natural resources of air, water, and land.

Our drinking water comes from surface water in rivers and lakes and from groundwater several feet below the surface. Rain, snow, and surface water slowly seep into the ground and become trapped in spaces within the rocks as groundwater. Our water resources can easily be polluted by waste and garbage, by fertilizers from farms, and by chemicals from factories. Geologists called hydrologists study surface water and groundwater to find out where pollution comes from and how to clean it up.

Acid rain is another pollution problem of concern to geologists. The air we breathe contains small amounts of acids and ozone (an oxygen compound), most of which result from

automobile exhaust and burning fossil fuels. The more we pollute the air, the more acidic it becomes, and this harms trees, fish, and even building stones. Geochemists are trying to learn how acid rain affects water, soil, and plants, and geologists are also working to reduce the amount of acids produced when coal and petroleum are burned.

Geologists also work in factories that refine earth materials such as iron ore, which is used to make steel. Others help develop synthetic materials as a substitute for natural minerals and rocks. Some geologists become gemologists and work with valuable gemstones. Still others are hired by banks which invest in geology-related companies. Some geologists work in schools or museums, studying and teaching people about the earth.

Some people practice civil geology. This is the geology needed to plan highways, bridges, and buildings. If you were a civil geologist you might help someone find the best place to drill a well for water. Civil geologists work with engineers and architects to design buildings that can withstand earthquakes, landslides, or other geological catastrophes.

Geologists will be needed for many years to help us use our planet wisely.

Glossary

Adobe (uh-DOE-bee) A mixture of clay and straw, molded into bricks and used as a building material.

Agate (AG-it) A variety of quartz with bands of different colors.

Alabaster (AL-uh-bas-ter) A variety of gypsum, usually forming rocks composed of small, white grains, and used as a building stone.

Alloy A combination of two or more metals.

Amethyst (AM-uh-thist) A purple variety of quartz.

Apatite (AP-uh-tite) A mineral that has a composition similar to a substance in bones and teeth.

Asbestos (az-BES-tus) A general term used to describe several fibrous minerals. Asbestos was once used for insulation because it is fireproof.

Aventurine (a-VEN-chu-REEN)   A red or green variety of quartz.

Background radiation   The natural energy produced by small amounts of radioactive elements in the rocks of the earth's crust.

Basalt (buh-SALT)   An igneous volcanic rock, usually dark in color and very fine-grained because it cools quickly and solidifies near the earth's surface. The ocean crust is mostly basalt.

Beryl (BER-uhl)   A mineral whose varieties include the gemstones emerald and aquamarine.

Bloodstone   A variety of quartz with a mottled green and red color.

Bort   A black diamond made of many microscopic grains.

Cabochon (KAB-uh-shawn)   A smooth, dome shape; some gemstones are cut into this shape.

Calcite (KAL-site)   A mineral found in many sedimentary and metamorphic rocks.

Calcium (KAL-see-um)   An element found in many minerals, including calcite, as well as in bones and teeth.

Carbon (KAR-bun)   An element. Graphite and diamond are minerals made of carbon.

Carbon 14   Radioactive atoms of carbon used to determine the age of rocks.

Carbuncle (KAR-bun-kul)   The name used in ancient times to refer to any red gemstone.

Cenozoic (se-ne-ZO-ic) **Era**   The present geological era, which began 66 million years ago.

Ceramic   Clay or other fine-grained combinations of minerals exposed to high temperatures.

Chalcedony (kal-SED-eh-nee)   The general term used for opaque varieties of quartz.

Chalcopyrite (KAL-keh-PIE-rite)   An important ore of copper; a mineral with metallic luster and a brassy, green-gold color.

Chalk   A fine-grained variety of calcite made of the shells of microscopic animals.

Chert   A variety of fine-grained quartz.

Cinder   A rock-like material full of small holes. It is an industrial waste produced by burning coal. Easily mistaken for volcanic rock. Also called clinker.

Cleavage (KLEE-vij)   The characteristic of some minerals to break along weaknesses in their structure, producing flat surfaces.

Cleavage rhombs (KLEE-vij ROMS)   A "lopsided box" shape, typical of the cleavage of certain minerals, especially calcite.

Clinker   *See* cinder.

Coal   The remains of ancient plants transformed by heat and pressure into black rock.

Conchoidal (kon-COY-dul) **fracture**   The characteristic of some minerals to show small, semicircular grooves on their broken surfaces that resemble seashells.

Concrete   A building material made of gravel, heat-treated limestone, water, and other rock material.

Concretion (kon-KREE-shun)   A lump of mineral, usually chert, calcite, hematite, or limonite, found inside sedimentary rocks. Water in the sediments deposits minerals around a grain of sand or piece of shell.

Conductor   A substance, such as a metal, that lets electrical current pass easily.

Conglomerate (kon-GLOM-er-it)   A sedimentary rock made of gravel-sized or larger pieces of sediment, rocks, minerals, or plant or animal remains, cemented together by finer-grained quartz, calcite, or hematite.

Continents   The seven large land masses of the earth: Africa, Antarctica, Asia, Australia, Europe, North America, and South America.

Continental crust   The part of the earth's crust that makes up the continents.

Core   The center portion of the earth's interior, made of the metals iron and nickel. The inner part of the core is solid; the outer part is molten.

Corundum (kor-UN-dum)   A mineral whose gem varieties are ruby and sapphire.

Crust   The outermost, rocky portion of the earth, less than 50 miles thick in most places. The crust makes up the continents and the floor of the oceans.

Crystal (KRIS-tul)   A solid substance with a regular arrangement of atoms. A crystal has smooth, flat faces that meet in sharp edges and corners.

Crystallization (kris-tu-lih-ZAY-shun)   The process by which crystals are formed. Crystallization includes the solidification of an igneous rock from magma and the formation of a mineral crystal out of water or within a rock under extreme heat and pressure.

Cuprite (KYOOP-rite)   A red mineral made of copper and oxygen. Cuprite is an ore of copper.

Delta   The accumulation of sediment at the mouth of a river, where it enters a lake or sea.

Diamond   The hardest mineral, with a hardness of 10 on the Mohs scale. It is made of carbon.

Diamond pipe   *See* kimberlite pipe.

Dolomite (DOL-uh-mite)   A mineral similar to calcite, but which does not fizz in cold, dilute acid.

Dolostone (DOL-uh-stone)   A rock made mostly of dolomite.

Earthquake   Vibration of the earth caused by the movement of magma, the earth's crust, or of continental plates.

Element   The purest form of matter. Every atom is an element.

Emerald (EM-er-uld)   The gem variety of beryl.

Erosion (ee-RO-zhun)   The process that wears away rock on the earth's surface through the movements of wind, water, and ice.

Facet (FAS-it)   A smooth, flat surface of a gemstone created by breaking, sawing, or grinding.

Fault   A zone within the earth's crust along which the rocks on either side have moved in opposite directions. Faults can be inches or hundreds of miles long.

Flint   A variety of fine-grained quartz, usually dark in color. It was used to make primitive tools and to create sparks for fires.

Fluorite (FLURE-ite)   A mineral that grows in box-shaped crystals; found mostly in sedimentary rocks.

Folding   Bends or wrinkles in metamorphic rocks produced by the shifting of the earth's crust. Sedimentary rocks occasionally contain folds formed when the sediments were still wet and soft, but these are not as regular as the folds in metamorphic rocks.

Fool's gold   Minerals such as pyrite or chalcopyrite that look like gold.

Fossil   The remains or imprint of ancient plants or animals, such as a shell, a bone, or a leaf impression in stone.

Fossiliferous (fah-se-LIF-er-us)   Any sedimentary rock that contains many fossils.

Fracture (FRAK-chur)   An irregular surface produced when a mineral breaks randomly, and not along a smooth cleavage plane.

Garnet (GAR-nit)   A mineral found in metamorphic rocks; usually deep red in color.

Gem   A mineral that is beautiful, durable, and rare.

Geode (JEE-ode)   A rounded lump of rock, usually made of quartz, that forms in a cavity in sediments. Many geodes are partly hollow and are lined with agate or crystals.

Geologic (jee-uh-LA-jic) **time**   The divisions of the earth's 4½ billion-year history into blocks of time marked by major natural events.

Geologist (jee-AHL-uh-jist)   A scientist who studies the formation of the earth or other planets in our solar system.

Glacier (GLAY-sher)   A large mass of ice that remains throughout the summer months, and which moves under its own weight.

Gneiss (NICE)　A metamorphic rock with layers of various minerals.

Gold　A valuable metal mineral that is found in its pure form, as a native metal.

Granite (GRAN-it)　A coarse-grained, non-volcanic igneous rock, typically light-colored; contains feldspar and quartz, as well as amphibole, mica, or both.

Graphite (GRAF-ite)　A mineral made of carbon that has a metallic to greasy luster and low hardness; used as a lubricant and to make pencils.

Grit　A powdered solid used as an abrasive to grind or polish rocks and minerals.

Groundwater　The water found in rocks just beneath the surface of the earth.

Gypsum (JIP-sum)　A mineral found in some sedimentary rocks, and used to make plaster of Paris.

Hackly fracture　The characteristic of some minerals to break in a jagged, random way.

Halite (HAY-lite)　Rock salt, a mineral found in some sedimentary rocks.

Hematite (HEM-a-tite)　A mineral with a red streak. It is an important ore of iron.

Hydrothermal (hy-dra-THER-mul)　"Hot water"; the process by which minerals dissolved in hot water form solid deposits.

Ice Age　A time when glaciers cover large areas of the land. The most recent Ice Age began about two and a half million years ago and continues today.

Igneous rock (IG-nee-us)　A type of rock formed by the cooling and solidification of molten rock on (or beneath) the earth's surface.

Iridium (ir-ID-ee-um)   An element that is very rare on earth but slightly more common in meteorites.

Jasper (JAS-pur)   A variety of fine-grained quartz with a yellow or red color.

Kimberlite (KIM-bur-lite) **pipe**   The volcanic passage which carries rock, magma, gas, and sometimes diamonds from the earth's mantle to the surface.

Lapidary (LAP-eh-der-ee) **equipment**   Equipment used to cut and polish gems, minerals, and rocks.

Lava (LA-va)   Molten rock that reaches the surface of the earth.

Limestone   A sedimentary rock made mostly of calcite or dolomite.

Lodestone (LODE-stone)   A type of magnetite with very strong natural magnetic properties, used in early compasses for navigation.

Luster   The way a mineral reflects light.

Magma (MAG-muh)   Molten rock beneath the surface of the earth.

Magnetite (MAG-neh-tite)   A mineral with natural magnetic properties that will attract a magnet. It is an ore of iron.

Mantle (MAN-tul)   The middle region of the earth's interior, between the crust and the core.

Marble (MAR-bel)   A metamorphic rock formed by the transformation of limestone by heat and pressure.

Mesozoic (mez-uh-ZO-ik) **Era**   The era of the earth's history from 245 to 66 million years ago, when dinosaurs walked the earth.

Metamorphic (met-a-MOR-fik) **rock**   A type of rock produced when an igneous or sedimentary rock is transformed by heat and pressure within the earth.

Meteor (MEE-tee-ur)   An extraterrestrial object, such as an asteroid or comet, that enters the earth's atmosphere.

Meteorite (MEE-tee-ur-ite)   Part of a meteor that reaches the earth. Scientists believe that meteorites are fragments of former planets.

Mineral (MIN-er-uhl)   A solid substance found in nature but not made by living things. Minerals have a regular arrangement of atoms, and can form a crystal under proper conditions.

Mineraloid (MIN-er-uhl-oid)   A substance with mineral properties that is not a true mineral.

Mohs (MOZE) **scale**   A system devised by Friedrich Mohs to determine the hardness of a mineral relative to other minerals.

Native metal   A metal, such as gold, copper, or silver, that is found in its pure form, rather than combined with other elements.

Obsidian (ob-SID-ee-en)   Natural volcanic glass that forms when lava erupts and quickly cools.

Ocean crust   The portion of the earth's crust that forms the floor of the oceans. The ocean crust is made up mostly of the igneous rocks basalt and gabbro.

Ore   Rocks or minerals that contain metals which may be extracted.

Paleontologist (pay-lee-un-TA-luh-jist)   A geologist who studies fossils of plants and animals that lived long ago.

Paleozoic (PAY-lee-o-ZO-ic) **Era**   The era of earth history from 570 to 245 million years ago. During this era, the first plants and animals that resemble modern life forms developed.

Petrified (PET-rih-fyd) **wood**   The rock produced when a mineral (usually quartz) replaces the decaying tissue of a tree.

Piezoelectricity (pee-AY-zoh-el-ek-TRIH-sih-tee)   The property of some minerals, such as quartz, to produce a small electrical charge when pressure is applied.

Plate tectonics (tek-TAHN-iks)   The theory that explains the origin of earth-quakes, volcanoes, and mountains in terms of the movements of huge areas of land, or plates, across the surface of the earth.

Precambrian (pre-CAM-bre-in) **Era**   The era of earth history from the formation of the planet 4½ billion years ago to the beginning of familiar life forms 570 million years ago.

Pumice (PUM-iss)   A rock made of volcanic ash; full of holes made by escaping gas bubbles.

Pyrite (PY-ryt)   Fool's gold; a mineral with metallic luster and a brassy yellow color, sometimes mistaken for gold.

Quartz (KWARTS)   The most common mineral in the earth's crust. It is made of silicon and oxygen, and can be found in many colors and forms.

Quartzite (KWARTS-ite)   A metamorphic rock formed by the transformation of sandstone by heat and pressure.

Radioactive (ray-dee-oh-AK-tiv)   The property of some atoms to break apart, forming different atoms and releasing energy.

Radioactive decay   The breakdown of radioactive atoms.

Rhomb   *See* cleavage rhombs.

Rock   A solid made of one or more minerals, sometimes also containing fossils. Also called a stone.

Rubidium (roo-BID-ee-um) **87**   A radioactive element used to determine the age of rocks.

Sandstone   A sedimentary rock made of sand-sized pieces of mineral and rock.

Schist (SHIST)   A metamorphic rock containing individual mineral grains large enough to see. Most schists have parallel layers of mica, amphibole, or talc, along which the rock splits apart.

Sediment (SED-ih-ment)   Pieces of rocks and minerals broken down by erosion; made of gravel, sand, mud, and plant and animal remains.

Sedimentary (sed-ih-MEN-ter-ee) **rock**   A type of rock made of sediments or by the deposit of minerals by water.

Seismograph (SYZ-mo-graf)   A device that measures the vibrations produced by earthquakes.

Semiconductor   A material that lets some, but not all, of an electric current pass through it. Also, an electronic device that controls the passage of an electric current.

Shale   A sedimentary rock made of fragments of minerals and rocks too small to be seen.

Silica (SIL-ih-kuh)   A compound of silicon and oxygen. Quartz is a form of silica.

Silicon (SIL-ih-kon)   An element that combines with oxygen to form quartz, and with other elements to form many different minerals.

Slag   Synthetic glass produced as a waste material from the smelting of iron ore. It is easily confused with volcanic glass.

Slate   A metamorphic rock made of fragments of minerals and rocks too small to be seen. It is usually formed by the metamorphism of shale.

Soapstone   A variety of the mineral talc, usually white, pale pink, or green, that is soft enough to be carved.

Superconductor   A ceramic compound that offers virtually no resistance to electrical current.

Synthetic (sin-THEH-tik) **mineral**   A substance with the properties of minerals, made in a laboratory.

Talc   The softest mineral, with a hardness of 1 on the Mohs scale.

Travertine   *See* tufa.

Tufa (TOO-fah)   A type of calcite that forms from natural hot or cold springs; also called travertine.

Tuff   An igneous rock made of volcanic ash.

Volcanic porphyry (vahl-KAN-ik POOR-fer-ee)   An igneous rock made of large mineral grains or crystals surrounded by rock with mineral grains too small to see.

Volcano (vahl-KAY-no)   A large hill or mountain built by the eruption of lava and ash.

YAG   A synthetic mineral (yttrium aluminum garnet) similar in structure to natural garnet; used in "ruby" lasers.

For More Information

Geology Illustrated. John S. Shelton. San Francisco: W. H. Freeman and Co., 1966. A good introduction to geological concepts illustrated with photos taken from the air by the author, a geologist and pilot.

It Began with a Stone. Henry Faul and Carol Faul. New York: John Wiley and Sons, 1983. A history of geology from the stone age to the age of plate tectonics theories.

Krakatau, 1883. Tom Simkin and Richard S. Fiske. Washington, D. C.: Smithsonian Institution Press, 1983. An absorbing account of the eruption of Krakatau in the Pacific Ocean and its aftereffects.

The Making of a Continent. Ron Redfern. New York: Times Books, 1983 (paperback 1986). The companion volume to the public television series of the same name. The vocabulary is advanced, but the pictures are without equal. Redfern tells the story of North America as well as of his own discovery of geology.

The Nemesis Affair. David M. Raup. New York: W. W. Norton and Co., 1986. An "insider's view" of the controversy over the possibility of an extraterrestrial cause for the mass extinction of the dinosaurs and other animals.

Our Modern Stone Age. Robert L. Bates and Julia A. Jackson. Los Altos, California: William Kauffman, Inc., 1982. The story of our non-metal resources: sand, gravel, clay, rocks, and minerals. For advanced readers, but includes addresses of state geological surveys and ordering information for visitor guides to mines prepared by the U.S. Bureau of Mines.

Rocks and Minerals. Dr. R.F. Symes. New York: Alfred A. Knopf, 1988. A color picture book for primary to intermediate level readers.

Start Collecting Fossils. Ted Daeschler.

Philadelphia: Running Press, 1988. An illustrated introduction to fossil hunting, complete with a package of real fossils.

Volcano: The Eruption of Mt. St. Helens. Staff of *The Daily News*, Longview, Washington, and *The Journal-American*, Bellevue, Washington. Longview, Washington: Longview Publishing Company, 1980. Primarily a picture book about the most famous volcano in the continental U.S.

Volcanoes. Robert Decker and Barbara Decker. San Francisco: W. H. Freeman and Co., 1981. A good but somewhat advanced introduction to volcanoes and their role in plate tectonics; abundant black-and-white photos.

Selected References

The following books are listed in *Selected References on Rocks, Minerals, and Gem Stones*, a bibliography compiled by the United States Geological Survey. The complete list is available free by writing: U.S. Geological Survey, Geologic Inquiries Group, 907 National Center, Reston, VA 22092.

GENERAL INTEREST

Color Encyclopedia of Gemstones (2nd edition). J.E. Arem. New York: Van Nostrand Reinhold, 1987.

The Magic of Minerals—110 Color Photographs by Olaf Medenbach. Olaf Medenbach and Harry Wilk. New York: Springer-Verlag, 1986.

Rocks and Minerals. G.S. Fichter. New York: Random House (Audubon Society Beginners Guide Series), 1982.

Simon and Schuster's Guide to Gems and Precious Stones. Kennie Lyman, ed. New York: Simon and Schuster, 1986.

FIELD GUIDES

The Audubon Society Field Guide to

North American Rocks and Minerals. C.W. Chesterman. New York: Alfred A. Knopf, 1979.

Dig It! A Directory of Fee-Basis Rock Collecting Sites Open to Amateurs (7th edition). C.E. Kindler. Philadelphia: Carol E. Kindler, 1986.

Gem Stones of the United States. Dorothy Schlegel. Seattle: Shorey, 1957 (reprinted 1975).

Lapidary Journal (periodical); annual April issue, "The Rockhound Buyer's Guide." San Diego: Lapidary Journal.

Mineral, Fossil and Rock Exhibits and Where to See Them (2nd edition). W.H. Matthews, III. Alexandria, Virginia: American Geological Institute, 1977.

Prospecting for Gemstones and Minerals (revised edition). John Sinkankas. New York: Van Nostrand Reinhold, 1970.

Suburban Geology—An Introduction to the Common Rocks and Minerals of Your Back Yard and Local Park. Richard Headstrom. Englewood Cliffs, New Jersey: Prentice-Hall, 1985.

Index

You'll find additional information in the Glossary, p. 107.

About the Author

LeeAnn Srogi earned her Ph.D.in geology from the University of Pennsylvania, and has taught there and at Smith College in Massachusetts. A native of suburban Detroit, she has been a rockhound since childhood, when she led her parents on field trips to gravel pits and quarries. She studies igneous and metamorphic rocks in New England, Pennsylvania, and Delaware. She resides in Pennsylvania.

The Running Press

START COLLECTING Series

Great New Ways To Begin Lifetime Hobbies

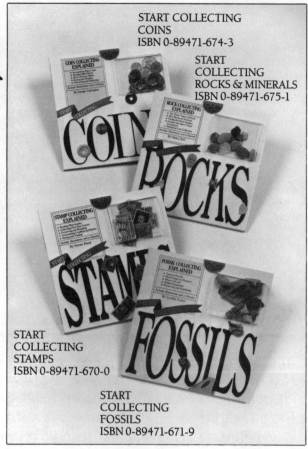

START COLLECTING COINS
ISBN 0-89471-674-3

START COLLECTING ROCKS & MINERALS
ISBN 0-89471-675-1

START COLLECTING STAMPS
ISBN 0-89471-670-0

START COLLECTING FOSSILS
ISBN 0-89471-671-9

Each edition of the *Start Collecting* series contains a book that shows you how to begin your own collection, together with an assortment of genuine collector's pieces to get you started.

Each complete set is only $9.95 and is available from your local bookstore.

Choose one or try them all – pick the hobby that's right for you!

If your bookstore does not have the edition you want, ask your bookseller to order it for you.